The
Funny Money Game

The
Funny Money Game

Andrew Tobias

First published in Great Britain by
Michael Joseph Limited
52 Bedford Square
London WC1

1972

7181 1074 9

Set and printed in Great Britain by
Tonbridge Printers Ltd
Peach Hall Works, Tonbridge, Kent
in Garamond eleven on twelve point
on paper supplied by P. F. Bingham Ltd
and bound by Dorstel Press,
at Harlow, Essex

To Maggie, who heightened the highs
and cushioned the downs;

And to Eloy, who is as important a
human being as an American businessman,
though it wouldn't seem so.

Acknowledgements

Among the people who offered ideas, criticism, and support for this book, I wish to thank these in particular: Rick McGraw, Livvy Floren, and Andrew Goodman, formerly of National Student Marketing Corporation; Professor John McArthur, Assistant Professor James Reece, Professor Theodore Levitt, and Russell Passarella of Harvard Business School; Stan Watson and Paul Zofnass of Harvard Law School; and Sheldon Zalaznick and Clay Felker, Editors of *New York* magazine.

A Word about the 1993 Edition

This book first appeared in the U.S. in 1971, and then in Britain (which accounts for the odd spellings in this edition, which was shot from that one).

In re-reading it, I was struck by how much "me-me-me" there is in it -- and reminded of the line about "hire a teen-ager -- while he still knows it all."

Anything that strikes you as wrong or dumb or pompous or sophomoric or bleeding-heart or holier-than-thou, you should please put down to youth. (If only my current transgressions were as easily explained away.)

Finally, it may be helpful to know in reading through this that a dollar in 1968 was the equivalent of about $4 today. And that 1968 was a long, long time ago.

Contents

CHAPTER ONE

I Think I Majored in Slavic

'I subscribe to the theory that one
obtains 94 percent of his education in
the dining hall.'
THOMAS W. STUART

The blackboards at Harvard Business School, 'West Point of
Capitalism,' are green, and they move up and down the walls
electrically. Each of the boards has its own switch on a control
panel, which also has a master switch to govern the flow
of electric power. According to one of our instructors, you
can tell whether a professor has tenure by how well he controls
those boards. Some men manipulate the switches with one
hand behind them as they face the class. Others rely on trial
and error. You've got to shut off the power at the right instant
because, like elevators, the boards keep going up or down a
few inches after you let the switch go. Tenured professors,
says our instructor, are board virtuosos.

Our finance professor faced us 63 aspiring Masters of
Business Administration, playing with the blackboards as he
helped us through our first class. Each of us, supposedly, was
a hot-ticket, or he wouldn't have gotten in. We were an
Olympic swimmer (athletes make good businessmen), a squad
of nuclear submariners (naval officers make captains of industry), a portfolio of millionaires-through-inheritance (money
makes money), a set of mathematical geniuses (training to

14

make two plus two make five), and assorted others like me, who had made it to the Business School in a variety of odd ways.

I had graduated from Harvard College in 1968 and had spent a couple of years out in the real world before entering Harvard Business School. A few weeks before business school started I was pictured inside a soap bubble on the cover of *New York* magazine. Judging from a remark our finance professor made to me near the end of the first class, I guessed he had read my article.

This first class promised to be dull. We were to scrutinize the financial statements of some company called Great Southwest Corporation. No pictures. Lots of footnotes and fine print. Sixty-three bored virtuosos.

Sixty-two, actually, because I confess those drab columns of numbers had caught my interest. I wasn't sure what they meant, but I was suspicious. As the blackboards climbed up and down the wall, it developed that Great Southwest was a subsidiary of a subsidiary of the Penn Central Company. Great Southwest had been acquiring subsidiaries of its own at a great rate. Its profits and stock price had been zooming. It further developed that about two-thirds of those profits were explained in a footnote and were illusory at best – and that the entire statement could be viewed as a huge joke at the expense of the public.

The professor wheeled around to me and asked, 'Does *that* sound familiar, Mr Tobias?'

As an undergraduate I majored in Slavic Languages and Literatures, which is to say I learned a smattering of Russian and read a lot of Russian novels in English. I graduated with honours, which is to say I squeezed into the top two-thirds of the class. I wasn't a very serious student because I quickly found an extracurricular activity much more exciting than studying: Business. (I am afraid I would have found almost any extracurricular activity more exciting than studying; it may be mere happenstance I am not now a Hari Krishna singer.)

15

During freshman-orientation week I bumped into a high school friend who was going to Harvard Student Agencies, Inc. (HSA) to get a job. The last thing I wanted to get involved with was business. The same high school trip to the Soviet Union that had generated my interest in Slavic languages and literatures had slid my self-image well to the left of nasty businessman, somewhere between respected do-gooder and adulated world-saver. But I saw no harm in earning a little money to secure a degree of independence.

My friend and I were immediately set to work hand-collating 5,000 14-page magazines at $1.75 an hour, which took all night. As we worked we learned that HSA was a student-run corporation designed to 'finance higher education through student enterprise.' It would have been a little cheaper to collate the magazine mechanically; however, this would have eliminated two term-time jobs. I felt out of place, coming from a family that was hardly disadvantaged; but I was pleased to be working for a business whose purpose was to provide student earnings rather than shareholder profits.

After we collated the magazine we delivered it to each door in the University. Two thousand doors, 400 flights of stairs, a $10 pay check. Then we were hired to help lay out ads for the next issue and to sell ads on commission. To get me started – I had never sold anything before – they told me to 'Go see Gardner Bradlee at the Cambridge Trust Bank.' I did, but was so frightened that Mr Bradlee had to lead me through my sales pitch and then, since I had forgotten the part about asking him to buy an ad, he had to ask me to let him buy a quarter of a page. This understanding gentleman, it turned out, was *President* of the bank, as well as Chairman of the Board of Harvard Student Agencies.

By the end of freshman-orientation week, I had earned about $100 – about $100 more than I had ever earned before. I was hooked. It was too late for studying to make its pitch for my primary interest. Although I didn't realize it all at once, I was changing ladders. In high school I had played the grade game, with whatever knowledge I may have picked

16

up a handy side-benefit. In college I played the business game, with whatever money I earned (about $10,000 over the four years) another handy side-benefit. The money did not provide me comforts I would otherwise have had to forego; my parents would willingly have provided reasonable comforts. Instead, it was the score in the game, and it was independence. This game was more fun than the grade game had been because it involved *real* playing pieces on a real-life playing board. Or fairly real, anyway.

Up to this point in my life I had been a Xerox of my big brother's elementary-school and high-school transcripts. But, as I entered Harvard three months after he had graduated with the highest possible academic honours, my subconscious must have been telling me the jig was up. My subconscious very much doubted my ability to remain competitive with brother's academic record, so it decided to change ballparks. The old apples and oranges ploy. It took a couple of years for my parents (the umpires, of course) fully to accept this deft footwork. My father complained at first that I was going to Harvard to obtain an education, not to earn money. I insisted that learning the perfectives of Russian verbs of motion was useless and boring and was delighted when an upperclassman advised me 'not to let my studies interfere with my education.' Luckily, Harvard is what a friend from the University of Cincinnati enviously calls a 'candy-ass school,' and what others call 'enlightened.' One is able to pass his courses with a minimum of dedication.

The August before my sophomore year I got a call from the HSA president offering me the chance to manage their little publishing company, which at the time had one title: *Let's Go, The Student Guide to Europe*. If I wanted the job, I would have to get on a plane right away to revise the chapters on Ireland, Switzerland, and Yugoslavia. I would have to visit scads of hotels, restaurants, and night spots and put up with all the excessive hospitality that a travel-guide editor is shown. Worse, I would probably have to do the same sort of thing the next couple of summers.

Sophomore and junior years I lived and breathed nothing

17

but *Let's Go, The Student Guide to Europe*. My salary of
$600 for the academic year worked out to something like 40c
an hour; however, we began to show a profit, and I got part
of that. We added three new titles to the line, took over half
HSA's basement office space, and had visions of outselling
Arthur Frommer's famous *$5-a-Day* travel guides in a few
years. Whenever I visited a bookstore I would make sure no
one was looking and then cover the stacks of Frommer's
books with copies of *Let's Go*.

I have only a vague recollection of going to classes. I
remember sitting in the back, opening the day's mail as quietly
as I could to avoid disturbing anyone. I would always try to
get involved with the lecture; but within the first few minutes
some key word would throw my mind away from Babel or
Bunin back to business. Oddly, there were never any key
words in my thoughts about business that threw my mind
back into the lecture.

One of the few clear memories I have of Slavic Languages
and Literatures was my encounter with Lufthansa (then billing
itself as 'The Airline That Says "Gesundheit" '). I was in
New York trying to sell $600 ads in *Let's Go* and gained
entry to the Director of Advertising for Lufthansa – presumably because she was curious to see what a nineteen-year-
old space salesman looked like. Her first question was, 'What
do you study?' and, upon finding out, her next comment was
something like, '*Khorosho, govoritye vsyo tol'ko porussky,
pozhaluysta.*' By a combination of ruble-red blushes and
enthusiastic '*Da's*' whenever she paused, I managed to hold
my own as she described her immigration to this country (I
suppose). And we got the ad.

We did not get an ad from Arthur Frommer – Mr *Europe
on $5-a-Day* – but meeting our competition at his office was
like being on their side in capture-the-flag. I was hoping he
would advertise his books and tours in *Let's Go*, even though
his advertising manager told me that 'Mr Frommer eats *Let's
Go* for breakfast,' (?) which I took as a bad sign. I knew that
early in its history, when *Let's Go* jumped on the Frommer
band-wagon, some of the student editors had used Frommer's

guide to 'discover' hotels and restaurants for *Let's Go*. Whatever he had had for breakfast, Mr Frommer was exceedingly warm and entertaining over lunch. (I must have been the only salesman in New York whose lunches were paid for by prospective clients.) I decided our competition was formidable: A brilliant graduate of Yale Law, brimming with energy; but friendly. He hinted at a job possibility after I graduated.

Senior year I was President of HSA, which is not as grand as it sounds because HSA is really run by the full-time (adult) General Manager. Whenever the President and General Manager agree, the President is in charge; whenever they disagree, the General Manager takes over. (This is perhaps why HSA has managed to survive so long.)

HSA provided students with good business experience, but enjoyed some rather unrealistic advantages that probably had more to do with our limited success than we cared to admit. Our bartending, information-gathering, and computer-programming services had the support of 70,000 enthusiastic alumni in Massachusetts. Our class-ring, linen, charter-flight, birthday-cake, and refrigerator-rental businesses all enjoyed University-enforced monopolies. All our businesses benefited from the availability of bright minds and athletic bodies at $2 an hour, non-union. Business school professors and bank presidents served on our Board of Directors without fee. And the Harvard name didn't hurt, either.

Even if our business successes were not entirely attributable to shrewd management, they made good press – another terrific advantage. Local media were forever plugging our services. Hugh Downs inflicted me and *Let's Go* on 'Today' show viewers for twenty-five minutes one February morning. I believe I went on at around a quarter-past five. That's how I felt, anyway. The peacock preceded me in living colour; I was scared to death. The next morning's mail brought 128 orders for the book and one hate postcard – something about seeing America first. *Newsweek* ran an article called 'The Campus Entrepreneurs,' and *The New York Times* ran 'Student Business Big Business Now.' Conservative publications like *This Week* magazine (R.I.P.) and *Reader's Digest* saw a chance to refresh their SDS-weary readers with Horatio Alger pieces like 'How To Earn (a Lot of) Money in College,' condensed from a book HSA published, and 'How To Succeed in Business Before Graduating,' condensed from a Princeton-based effort.

The logical place for someone with my interests to go after college seemed to be business school. Although Harvard Business School admits about a fourth of its students fresh out of college, applicants are advised to spend a couple of years in the real world first to make B-School more meaningful. My reason for not going straight to B-School was different: I couldn't bear two more years of academia. After sixteen years of school I was so eager to enter the real world, tackle real problems, and earn real money I didn't even attend my own graduation. Now, looking back on the last two years through my B-School window, they seem just a little unreal....

There I was in my senior year, star of the 'Today' show, quoted in *This Week, Newsweek,* and *The New York Times,* and armed with four years of Slavic Languages and Literatures. Who needed business school? I spent April 1968 sitting by the phone waiting to be called to run the World Bank or Pan American Airways. Like other student entrepreneurs I will mention later, I was ready to leave the unreal ivory-towered world of business to make my fortune in the unreal real world of business. At first I thought it should take about ten years to make a fortune; but when I learned that most self-respecting student entrepreneurs expected to do it in three to five years, max, I raised (lowered?) my sights.

I had not abandoned my world-saving fantasies, by the way. I had merely adopted the following Great Rationalization: The only way to make a dent is from a position of power. I am not cut out for politics, but I like business. If I can learn to administer a multimillion-dollar business project, then perhaps I can slide into the government bureaucracy at a fairly high level, say in HEW, and administer a multimillion-dollar government project. What's more, as I happen to enjoy business more than tutoring retarded kids, it should be acceptable for me to earn and donate money to pay the salary of someone who prefers tutoring to business. I admit I have never been 100% satisfied with this rationalization.

CHAPTER TWO

Corporate Identity Search

Take a ride on the Penn Central
Railroad. If you pass Go, collect $200.

When the phone did ring, it was Dan Goldenson, the fellow from Princeton behind *How To Succeed in Business Before Graduating*. He gently broke the news about McNamara getting the World Bank and Halaby taking over Pan Am, and then offered me the Vice-Presidency of Resource Publications, Inc., which had brought *him* success in business before graduating from Princeton in 1966, and was bringing him lots more now. He had just sold Resource Publications to Gulf + Western Industries – I couldn't remember whether that was oil or rail-roads, but I knew it was good – adding about two-hundredths of one percent to G+W's $1.6 billion of sales.

I packed my belongings into my Acapulco-blue Mustang and moved to Princeton.

On Graduation Day, 1968, I was in the midst of my second month as Vice-President of G+W's tiniest subsidiary. I asked Harvard to mail me my diploma and to convey my regrets to our Commencement speaker, His Excellency the Shah of Iran.

Resource had started as an annual magazine distributed free through college placement offices to graduating engineers in New Jersey. The clever business twist to this publication was that the ads were the articles. Companies around New Jersey who wanted to attract young engineers were asked to submit full-page 'profiles' of the opportunities they had to offer. For $150, Resource would publish the profiles in its magazine. Resource did not have to support the writing and production costs of nonrevenue-producing articles, like most magazines. Virtually every page paid for itself. Because the companies were asked to follow a standard text format, the magazine appeared to have no ads rather than being nothing but ads.

By the time I arrived, Dan had already expanded this concept to twenty-two regional magazines, covering the whole country. Large national advertisers would place their profiles in all editions; smaller companies would choose the regions nearest them. There were 1,500 profiles in all!

Having multiplied one region by twenty-two, the next step, clearly, was to multiply one career (engineering) by, say, twelve – or 264 magazines in all. I have since learned to be wary of Clear Next Steps and Exponential Growth Curves. Not to mention how frightened I have become of Even If We Attain Only a Fraction of This Projection.

Gulf+Western, I discovered, was neither oil company nor railroad, but 'conglomerate.' That is, it owned about forty diverse companies that had nothing to do with oil or railroads – and very little to do with each other, for that matter. Top management spent most of its time trying to acquire other companies, but usually called it merging, so the other companies would not feel victimized. Most of the acquisitions were accounted for on a 'pooling of interests' basis, so G+W could give the owners of the acquired companies some stock without their having to pay taxes on it and then lump the new companies' sales and earnings into G+W's statements as though they had always been one company. At the age of twenty-four, Dan had traded Resource Publications for what *Fortune* reported to be $1 million of G+W stock. The exact amount would depend on the profits Resource produced over the succeeding three years; there was a strong incentive for Dan to produce. Dan's stock was 'unregistered,' which meant he couldn't sell it for a couple of years, though he could borrow against it.

Like most key G+W executives, Dan also had a 'qualified stock option.' Say you have an option on 5,000 shares at $42, he explained. You wait until the stock climbs to, say, $53 and then buy it from the company at $42 and sell it on the market at $53. I calculated that in such a situation you would make $5,000 for every point G+W stock rose above $42. There was also something about paying capital-gains tax instead of income tax. Although you would have to wait two years before you could exercise your stock option, that would give the stock, already up to $50 a share, time to appreciate still more. I was fascinated by the idea of stock options and more than a little impressed by what my leader had been able to build for himself in such a short time. You might even say envious.

Gulf+Western management were aware how few people knew anything about their company. They wanted to develop an exciting new image, which they hoped would make their stock more attractive to investors. So they retained some 'corporate-identity specialists' to develop a new image. I was appointed corporate-identity liaison for Resource and got to ride the Penn Central into New York for the G+W corporate-identity day at the Biltmore Hotel. The morning was devoted to a presentation by Lippincott & Margulies, the leader among corporate-identity specialists, who showed slides of the plastic surgery they had done on RCA. Now you know what happened to the dog that used to howl into the RCA victrola. We heard Gulf+Western President, Jim Judelson, explain how G+W had started as a small auto-parts distributor about a dozen years back, how he and Chairman Charlie Bludhorn had acquired a lot of seemingly unrelated companies, how it was important to have a good corporate identity, how they were shelling out a small fortune to develop the new G+W logo, and how we had better like it.

At lunch I learned that a strong corporate identity was only one aspect of 'synergy.' Webster's defines synergy as 'Co-operative action of discrete agencies such that the total effect is greater than the sum of the two effects taken independently . . .' In other words, when you combine Resource Publications with Paramount Pictures, a zinc-mining outfit, and an auto-parts distributor, $1+1+1+1=7$. (Don't you see?) The synergy, of course, is more than enough to support the massive new administrative, legal, accounting, and public-relations overhead – like a $50,000 logo – needed to hold the whole thing together.

In 1968 synergy was Wall Street's favourite word. Pythagoras ('The whole is the sum of its parts.') was out; Sperry Rand ('One day we lift a log. The next day we shave a face. We're synergistic.') was in.

After lunch the men from Lippincott & Margulies were shuffled out and the corporate identifiers who had developed the new look for G+W were shuffled in. The new logo was unveiled. Someone near me whispered disapproval; someone else whispered something about going into the corporate-identity business if that was all there was to earning such fat fees. But generally everyone behaved with enthusiastic in-difference as they puffed on the cigars, manufactured by a G+W subsidiary, that were handed out after lunch. Someone asked whether it was pronounced 'Gulf plus Western' or 'Gulf and Western.' Someone else asked why it was pro-nounced 'Gulf and Western' when it was written 'Gulf+ Western.' Others asked what colours they would be allowed to use in printing the new logo, whether they should get rid of all their old stationery, and so on. I went back to Princeton with all the answers.

Meanwhile, as I was getting my introduction to the inner workings of Big Business, my $15,000 salary was a source of endless ego gratification. And at night I could dream of my 25% share in incremental after-tax profits. Too much? In light of my youthful leader's good fortune, I felt comfortable with both title and compensation. Too little? I had been pul-ling down what came to $1.55 an hour as President of HSA, so this was a 400% raise. After covering modest living expenses, my salary left plenty of room for gimmickry, guilt cheques, and gambling.

Gimmickry: When I wasn't called 'Motor Mouth' in

25

college, I was called 'Super Consumer.' A typical expenditure in Princeton was $125 for a four-foot lava lamp (formless white gook rising and falling in a red liquid-filled glass cylinder), a gift so garish that, 25th anniversary or no, my parents refused to have anything to do with it. It became one of the attractions of my own apartment instead. More of the lava lamp, and the decadent companion pieces that joined it, later.

Guilt Cheques: My consistent good fortune and affluence have always bothered me as being a little out of place in a country with twenty-four million people classified by the government as poor, in a world where roughly two billion people, most of whom work harder than I do, are malnourished and miserable. So I adopted Eloy Velez in Ecuador through the Foster Parents Plan and wrote assorted guilt cheques each month to a variety of social and political groups. Part of my Great Rationalization.

Gambling: This one requires a little background. A fellow student entrepreneur had started a mutual-fund sales company and was training flocks of students to pass the licensing exam so they could sell their friends and relatives mutual funds. It was clearly only a matter of three to five years before he would have his fortune. One of his flock got me to buy the Ivest Fund at about $17, showing me its impressive performance curve and stressing the advantages of a 'medium-sized' fund. In deciding to trade my GM for Ivest, I reasoned that 'it would be wildly arrogant for me, a part-time amateur, to hope to do better than a team of proven experts.' Though I don't think much of Ivest (I lost $8\frac{1}{2}\%$ immediately – the fee charged by the fund to manage my money – and another 15% before I sold it), would that I had followed my reasoning all the way through! What a triumph it would have been to lose as little as Ivest!

But I was exposed to great temptations. One of the guys in the office was playing 'puts and calls' and explained how this 'leveraged' his money. For example, he explained, instead of spending $5,000 to buy 100 shares of some stock at $50, you can usually buy a 'call' on 100 shares for a few hundred dollars. Then, if the stock goes up within the time limit of the call (six months is typical), you can exercise your call by buying the stock at $50 and selling it on the market at the higher price. Just like buying a short-term stock option. You buy a 'put' instead of a call if you think the stock is going to go down. I hope you don't understand that explanation, because I wouldn't want you to get burned the way I did.

Anyhow, every lunch hour this fellow would walk up Princeton's Nassau Street to the local office of Tout, Ticker, Dicker & Churn, I think it was, to punch out all his different holdings on the Quotron. He showed me how to work the Quotron, and I was itching to own things to punch out.

Another fellow in the office got daily phone calls from his broker, and the news was usually good. Across the hall there was a little company selling a combination life-insurance–mutual-fund package that was about to go public. Sometimes in the evening a Blue Cross salesman who used to work for Dan would come by to trade stock tips. He had bought a thing called Omega Equities at 50c a share (that made a lot of sense to me – almost no risk at all, since it could only go down half a point at the most, and had tremendous 'upside' potential) and was kicking himself for not having bought it when it was 25c. When he first told us about Omega, it was up to $5, but he still recommended buying it. Before the summer was out it hit $25. This kind of astronomical growth didn't make economic sense to me. But there it was, confirmed in print every day in the papers and the 'Pink Sheets,' where quotations are listed for the many companies too small to be traded on one of the exchanges and traded 'over-the-counter' instead. I was no fool. I wasn't going to pass up opportunities like this any longer. My only regret was that the average man on the street, who could have used some capital gains far more than I, had neither the hot tips nor the capital to get started. 'The rich get richer...' I thought guiltily.

I sold my Ivest, took my just-turned-21 $3,000 inheritance

and part of my salary, and began to place my bets. My dad's broker had hot tips on Electronics Assistance, which I picked up at $25, and Coburn Credit, which I snagged at the same price. These were both on the American Exchange, which seemed awfully conservative to me, but I was willing to have a few blue chips amidst my rapidly churned portfolio of over-the-counter issues. My own broker, brother-in-law of my good friend Humphrey, who had just finished Princeton and Harvard Business, was one of the top men at Dewey, Scrume & Howe. He put me on to Cognitronics at $60. Dan had ridden Prudential Resources from $30 to $60 and expected it to break $100, so I bought a little of that. I didn't know anything about the activities of these companies, but I knew they were glamour stocks recommended by skilled, successful investors. The one issue I bought on a fluke, without anyone's recommendation, was National Student Marketing Corporation (NSMC). Just before leaving Harvard I had noticed a prospectus for this new issue and read it. It was the first prospectus I had ever read. I was intrigued because I had had some minor contacts with the young President of the company, Cort Randell.

I started gambling when, unbeknown to me, the economy was at its most unreal. The Dow Jones industrial average was floating in the 900s, while speculative over-the-counter issues were going wild. Since everyone had a general theory about the market, I quickly formulated my own: Firsts always take ages, seconds are quick to follow – the first telephone took many years to develop, the second was produced days later. Therefore, since the Dow Jones had inched its way up towards its first 1,000, it would shortly break through and rise rapidly to 2,000. It was a combination of resistance-level theory and my solid wishful thinking.

Any bright young man those days, it seemed, could make his fortune in one of two ways: Start a company with a jazzy name and ambitious plans and then (a) like Dan, sell it to a merger-crazed conglomerate (into which category most public companies, one began to suspect, apparently fell); or (b) like Cort Randell, take it public. Everyone knew that new stock issues were hot, so everyone bought them, so they went up, so they were indeed hot, so everyone bought them, and they went up still farther. (Most stock-market movements, my latest theory contends, are a series of self-fulfilling prophecies.) In the case of Cort's NSMC, the stock was supposed to be offered to the public at $6 a share. In fact, demand for new issues was so strong it started trading at $14. For the fun of it I brought 20 shares the next day at $16, fully expecting it to settle back down.

Over the course of the summer there were four important developments:

1. Five light boxes joined my lava lamp.

2. Eloy, my Ecuadorian boy, entered the fifth grade weighing 65 pounds.

3. I began to lose interest in my job. It turned out that my major responsibility was to make about 1,000 WATS-line sales calls to last year's customers, who were not sure their ads with us had brought them any engineers, and who, with NASA cutting back, were not planning on hiring more engineers in the near future anyway, so why didn't I call back around this time next year? At Resource we had no monopoly, no faithful alumni. I missed the instant fame and success I had become accustomed to on campus. Improving Dan's profits was harder than I had thought it would be.

4. The market slumped and all my glamour stocks but one went down, so I sold them to buy new glamour stocks. After all, everyone told me to 'buy high and sell low.' Or was it the other way around? In any case, that's what I generally managed to do. I sold Electronics Assistance and Coburn on their way from $25 to $3, Cognitronics somewhere between $60 and $4, and Prudential Resources as it dropped from $60 to $5.

The one stock that performed for me was National Student Marketing. To my astonishment, instead of settling back from $16, where I bought it, it moved to $23 a couple of weeks later, so I bought 20 more shares and raced to the Pink Sheets at Tout, Ticker earlier and earlier each day. By the end of the summer I was going for lunch around 10:45. And by the time I actually went to NSMC in New York and visited Cortes Wesley Randell (What kind of name is that, I kept wondering? I knew a Puerto Rican named Cortes, two blacks named Wesley, and a Jew named Randell), I had bought still another 20 shares at $37.

CHAPTER THREE

Touch Me, Touch Me

Midas called himself a happy man,
but felt he was not yet quite so happy
as he might be. The very tip-top of
enjoyment would not be reached,
unless the whole world were to become
his treasure room, and be filled with
yellow metal which should be all his
own.

King Midas and the Golden Touch
NATHANIEL HAWTHORNE

I had first heard about Randell and NSMC in 1966 from an upperclassman in my house, Jeff Tarr, who was that year's most celebrated student entrepreneur. Tarr was arranging tens of thousands of blind dates by computer – Operation Match – and was appearing with Johnny Carson and Mike Douglas to publicize the venture. Unfortunately, practical problems of management, fulfilment, and promotion after the initial flood of free publicity kept Jeff from making a full-fledged fortune at 23, but he did manage to sell his business to some 'professionals.' Jeff told me that if I wanted to sell more *Let's Go* guidebooks, I should call Cort Randell. Cort's company had student reps putting up posters on campuses all over the country with pads of tear-off order forms for Operation Match, airline half-fare cards, and student-rate magazine subscriptions. Maybe he would be willing to put up posters for *Let's Go.*

31

Randell, then 30 years old, was hard to get hold of, so I knew he was important. A 'National' company headquartered in Washington (as it then was) sounded important. His office was on the same street as the White House, I noticed, and not 1297-A Pennsylvania Avenue, either. 2400. Obviously a fancy building, which meant high rent, which meant NSMC was prosperous.

When I did get to speak with Randell, he was awfully nice and enthusiastic. Certainly he had heard of *Let's Go* – and thought we were doing a fine job. He spoke very highly of Jeff and confirmed what I had by now gathered: Cort was selling so fast he could hardly fill the orders; his business was mushrooming; success, success, success.

He wanted me to call him Cort. He had been thinking of a poster with three student-oriented books offered (maybe one on avoiding the draft). Yes, he would operate on nothing more than a percentage of the money that was sent in, and it could be very profitable for both of us. Problem: Just how many copies of *Let's Go* could we supply how fast? Cort couldn't have a situation where we sold out and left 10,000 mail-order customers fuming. My eyes opened wide at the thought of such a sweet problem. He figured that the first 'poster wave,' as he called it, would sell anywhere from 5,000 to 20,000 books – but he had no way of limiting it. He would be very disappointed in *Let's Go*'s appeal if it could not sell 10,000 copies. (A twinge of doubt: Were we good enough for Cort Randell?) Naturally, if it sold well, there would be more poster waves.

I had the distinct impression that Cort Randell could not fail, that he had found the secret formula, and that whoever he touched would turn to gold. Touch me, touch me.

He had a lot of important projects to get going before he would be ready to launch the *Let's Go* campaign, but he would get in touch in the spring. Meanwhile, would I check on the supply end to be sure we could meet the orders. Apart from the prospect of a hyperbolic sales curve for *Let's Go* (Even If We Attained Only a Fraction of This Projection . . .), I was bubbling that the President of an obviously big and highly successful company was being so friendly and complimentary. He had won my vote.

Nothing ever came of my occasional phone conversations with Randell except a smouldering interest in his company. That's why I bought the stock. And then while I was working at Resource I happened to meet two student entrepreneurs at a party thrown by Dan's uncle, Leonard Goldenson, President of ABC. At the University of Pennsylvania's Wharton School of Finance, Tan Miller and Ed Swan had started CompuJob, which matched student résumés with company needs at the company's expense – a cross between Resource Publications and Operation Match. Since it worked on one campus, the Next Clear Step was to try it nationwide, multiplying it 2,000-fold. Cort bought out CompuJob, one of his first acquisitions, and Tan and Ed dropped out of Wharton to become two of his first lieutenants. When I met them, they were busily going nationwide for the fall of 1968 and owned NSMC stock valued at something like a million dollars each. I thought this was running a little faster than the three-to-five-year rules of entrepreneurial etiquette should allow.

Tan thought a twenty-one-year-old of my background could be doing a lot better than I was; and I let on that I might consider an offer. Tan and Cort were quick to figure that if Harvard Student Agencies did about $1 million in sales on one campus, then NSMC could realize healthy growth by starting similar organizations on the 2,000 campuses that had none. This would result in NSMC sales of $2 billion – or, to be conservative, let's halve that and call it an even billion. Surely, having run HSA, I was just the man to develop this end of NSMC's business. (At that time NSMC sales were about $3 million, so even if it took me five years to develop the 2,000 campuses I would still be playing an important part in Cort's plans.)

I tried to explain why such a plan could not be executed – and one glaring reason why NSMC should not execute it even if it could: After ten years HSA had reduced its cumulative operating loss to about $10,000. In other words, after ten years' work on 2,000 campuses NSMC might look forward to a cumulative operating loss of $20 million. Randell said we could learn from HSA's mistakes, realize economies of scale, and so on, and even if I couldn't follow *his* plan, he was confident I could build worthwhile business for NSMC some other way. True, NSMC would know better than to purchase a fleet of Ollie Orbit Mobile Ice Cream trucks (what a cold, wet summer that was for HSA) – but NSMC couldn't expect all of HSA's special advantages, either. After making efforts to get him to be realistic about what I could do for him, I again expressed interest in being made an offer. I felt rotten at the prospect of leaving Dan alone to make all those WATS-line sales calls and determined not to accept Cort's offer unless it proved really enticing. I felt Dan, having made his fortune, would understand my impatience to make mine.

Cort's offer: The same salary I was getting at Resource to cover living expenses in New York (headquarters were moving from Washington to New York), plus a 3,000-share option at $37,[1] which, he felt, would be worth $1 million in three to four years. I felt like explaining how that would fit my timetable nicely, but instead asked how the option would become so valuable. On the back of a huge Manila envelope, which I keep in the same drawer as my lava-lamp warranty and my Harvard diploma, Cort showed me how NSMC had tripled for the past three years, and how much my options would be worth if it kept growing at 250% a year (though, confidentially, they were shooting higher and had never failed to exceed a goal).

As I mentioned above, I was no fool, and in the back of my mind something told me this was all a little unreal. But no, some awfully distinguished firms seemed to attest to NSMC's good character: Lawyers were White and Case; auditors had been Arthur Andersen and were then (without even knowing the rest of the sentence, a Harvard Business School graduate would see red flags going up all over, but

[1] Throughout this book I have stated NSMC shares, earnings and stock prices on the basis of the original stock, unadjusted for either of the two-for-one splits. To convert to adjusted figures, multiply all shares by 4 and divide all earnings figures and stock prices by 4.

at the time I never thought to wonder why a company switched auditors) Peat, Marwick, Mitchell & Co. (more red flags, but I had never heard of Yale Express, and who then knew what was going on at Penn Central?). Furthermore, Cort's performance was not only documented in the Pink Sheets, it was being proclaimed in *Time* (May 31, 1968), as well:

'I don't know quite how it happened that I'm making $1,000,000 a month,' says Cortes Wesley Randell, thirty-two, a Washingtonian who is president and chief executive of National Student Marketing Corp. 'I just sit in the office and talk to people.'

Randell's fast-growing wealth, which he offhandedly understates, comes from stockholdings.... Since April 24, when the company brought out a public issue of its common stock, the price of its shares has jumped from $6 to $26.50 on the over-the-counter market. Accordingly, the value of Randell's 54% holding has swelled from $2,509,998 to just over $11 million.

Randell makes money through a network of 581 part-time campus representatives, who earn up to $4,000 a year distributing samples, doing market research and peddling fad items. Last year, for example, they sold 55,000 paper dresses in twenty-seven days for Mars Manufacturing Co., topped that by selling 100,000 personality and psychedelic wall posters (at $1 each) ...

Having written a thesis on 'How to Start a Small Business' while enrolled at the University of Virginia, Randell persuaded himself to follow his own prescription while he was working as a marketing manager for ITT in Chicago. The idea jelled during a debutante party in Newport. As he sailed up to the dock in his college roommate's yacht, he recalls, 'I decided I was getting behind.' In his spare time, he wrote a guide to collegiate summer jobs, then at a cost of $150 printed up posters advertising 'high-paying, fun-filled positions' and distributed them on four Wisconsin campuses. So many

35

orders poured in the first week that Randell quit his $12,500-a-year job and went into business for himself.

After reading that, I was ready to quit my $15,000-a-year job and go into business for Randell. But then, just to distort whatever sense of reality I may have had left completely out of proportion – and to give me a 100% absurd estimate of my own business value – I got a call from Dan Richard, of whom I had never heard, asking me to discuss Class, Inc., a student-marketing company he had recently started and would soon be taking public. Class, he explained, had the creativity NSMC lacked; was attracting some of Cort's best people; would share the vast student market with NSMC; would enjoy the same miraculous stock-market success (everyone knew new issues were hot and the youth market was hot, so everyone would buy Class, so it would indeed be hot...). Would I accept a vice-presidency, $19,500 annual salary, and 3,000 shares of the stock (not options, stock, that would be issued shortly at $15 a share) and go up to New York to take office space wherever I felt wisest and set up shop to compete with NSMC, proceeding with whatever projects I felt would make the most money the fastest – discussing major decisions, of course, with the Washington office? *Agh!* Who do you think I am? The Wizard of Oz? I decided not to let on to Richard that he was amending the Peter Principle: By accepting such an offer I would not have been rising to my lowest level of incompetency, but to about the second level from the top.

Richard had just printed a million and a half copies of the first issue of *Class, The Student Guide*, which several hundred colleges had agreed to accept free and distribute to students at registration. There were few paying advertisers. Gant had the back cover, and by coincidence there was a two-page article plugging Gant shirts. Bobbie Brooks had the inside back cover, and Dan told me he had grown up in the same orphanage with the President of Bobbie Brooks. Most of the remaining ninety-eight pages were taken up with mail-order ads for products ranging from stick-on Jack-Pot Fruitees (an original Class creation) to a false beard and moustache set.

These were ads which *Class* would run free in return for a percentage of whatever mail-order sales were produced. One ad invited students to send in plays, poetry, or pros (*sic*) which would be compiled as the first edition of an anthology. Another ad invited students to send in $1.95 for the anthology, not mentioning that it had not yet been written, edited, typeset, or printed. The editorial content was designed to be noncontroversial and generally plugged the mail-order products. It seemed to me the magazine was slanted to the eleven to fourteen age group.

Richard figured that paid advertisements would cover production costs of *Class* in the future, and that profits would come from mail orders. With so many products offered, he couldn't see the average copy producing less than $1 of sales – or $1.5 million from the first issue. Or was it $1 of profit? Whatever it was, I remember thinking he was off by a factor of about 100. Still, Even If He Attained Only a Fraction of His Projection . . .

Dan Richard, I decided, was not the solid, proven, no-nonsense businessman Cort Randell was. Even though he was offering a higher salary and actual stock, I decided NSMC was the more sensible way to go. True, Richard had an indoor swimming pool and a U.S. Congressman on his Board of Directors, and Cort did not (I later heard that this Congressman died in a Las Vegas hotel room under questionable social circumstances). But when Cort flew me to Washington he had me stay at the Mayflower ($27, plus a $5.50 breakfast); and when I visited the new NSMC offices in New York's Time-Life Building I found Connie Hess working there – the sister of my first high school girlfriend and daughter of Hess Oil. I know solidarity when I see it.

Meet four men driven by the Big Money. Dan Goldenson, a very gentle, generous soul, was driven by G+W's incentive formula: Each dollar Dan produced in profit jacked up the purchase price of his company. Dan was married in August 1968. The combination of a European honeymoon and anxiety over the welfare of his business produced a first-class case of mononucleosis. Cort was driven by the knowledge that every point he could raise NSMC stock was another half-million dollars of personal net worth. Cort married on September 15th, 1968, allowing himself only three days away from business for a honeymoon. Dan Richard was driven by the need to go public before enthusiasm for new issues and the youth market waned; to get his foot in the door before Cort sewed up the entire $435-billion youth market. I was driven by the thought that each day I stayed at Resource, NSMC stock went a little higher, raising the price at which my options would be pegged – essentially costing me about $3,000 a day. But could I leave to Dan, insignificant as my contribution was, the whole responsibility for Resource Publications, when he had mononucleosis? After all, Dan had been very good to me and I had been with him only four months.

My Mustang was too small to hold all the junk I had by then accumulated, so I rented a U-Haul van for the move to New York. The incredible stench along the New Jersey Turnpike (which even reached Princeton when the wind was right) seemed nasal proof of the economy's good health – rather than the country's illness as I discovered two years later.

CHAPTER FOUR

Harvard, Princeton, and Maybe Jail

Red-Headed Man to [Sherlock] Holmes:
'. . . For I had quite persuaded myself
that the whole affair must be some
great hoax or fraud. . . . It seemed past
belief that they would pay such a sum
for doing anything so simple. . . .'
Holmes to Watson: 'You see, Watson, it
was perfectly obvious from the first
that the only possible object of this
rather fantastic business . . . was to get
the not overbright pawnbroker out of
the way for a number of hours every
day. . . . The £4 a week was a lure
which must draw him, and what was it
to them, who were playing for
thousands?'
The Red-Headed League
The Adventures of Sherlock Holmes
SIR ARTHUR CONAN DOYLE

I found that New York was more expensive than Princeton
and decided to split expenses with my friend Humphrey, my
broker's brother-in-law, who had just begun work at another
prestigious firm on Wall Street. We signed a two-year lease
(hereinafter referred to as the goddamned lease) for an Upper

East Side apartment managed by one of New York's leading real-estate firms (hereinafter referred to as the goddamned landlord). The vagaries of New York rent controls being what they are, we were paying more for three rooms on the second floor with a view of a bicycle-rental shop than either Humphrey's parents (six large rooms overlooking Central Park) or mine (five on Fifth Avenue) paid for theirs. Of course, since Humphrey and I would have our fortunes within three to five years, we were not awfully concerned. What did irk, though, was the attitude of the landlord. You see, they were doing us a *big favour*, letting us live for two years in a little apartment for $10,000. Apartments are so scarce in Manhattan that tenants have to sign leases requiring them to obtain written permission from the landlord to put a picture on the wall, but expressly protecting the landlord from any penalty in case there happens to be no heat or water for a few days or weeks. You also need written permission to have a guest stay overnight. Of course, everyone ignores such provisions – but whenever the landlord decides to get nasty, you lose.

I didn't spend much time in the apartment, anyway. I had my own little office at NSMC on the thirty-fifth floor of the Time-Life Building with a phenomenal view of Wall Street and beyond. During the day you couldn't see much more than the dust kicked up by the foundation blasting going on directly in front of us. But there were some spectacular sunsets and (would you believe?) sunrises. I liked it best on late winter afternoons when it was already dark outside and all the lights were still on in the office buildings and on Broadway. Looking through my window from a window washer's point of view was somewhat less impressive. A modern desk and chairs, Touchtone phone receiver invariably attached to my left ear, and a framed lithograph hanging on the wall – it was D'Arcangelo's yellow hand pointing right, inside a red arrow pointing left. I still have it, only now it hangs on its side.

The first month was a little unnerving because I operated in a vacuum. No one reported to me and there was no one

40

available for me to report to. I nervously guessed that my job was to launch 2,000 campus businesses, which I knew was absurd, or else figure out some other way to boost earnings, which I sat and tried to do – though the whole situation smacked of *The Red-Headed League,* which I made a point of rereading. I would fill yellow pads with wild ideas, make eyes at the Statue of Liberty, call Humphrey to get a quote on our stock, and try to figure out how to spend the money from my option. By the end of that first month it was worth $130,000. I had only twenty-three months to wait before I could exercise it.

An important feature of options, I knew from Dan, was their treatment as capital gains instead of ordinary income. At the time, $770,000 of every additional $1 million you made in ordinary income or short-term capital gains went straight to the government (in theory, anyway), compared with only $250,000 of every million of long-term capital gains. So it made a difference and I wanted to find out just what the rules were. Cort, having granted about 100 options, was the logical one to ask. He said any capital gains I realized from the option were automatically considered long-term, because I had had to wait two years to exercise the option.

To my surprise, the chief financial officer – then Bernie Kurek, recruited by Cort from Thompson's Dairy – said you had to exercise your option and then hold the stock for six months before selling it in order to qualify for long-term capital gains. A bank would probably lend you money to buy the stock, especially if your option price was a lot lower than the going market value. Another company officer's guess was that you had to hold the stock for *three years* after exercising the option in order to get capital gains.

I solicited these divergent opinions in the early days of my employment. This was the first in the long series of jaw droppers I experienced with NSMC. You mean nobody had bothered to find out? Weren't the other option-holders curious to know whether they got to keep $230,000 or $750,000? Whether they had to borrow a fortune from the bank and pray

the stock stayed up for six months or three years? You mean
Cort Randell didn't know? I wasn't just asking whether our
medical plan covered wisdom teeth. Because of these options,
everybody had low salaries, by New York-executive standards.
Everybody lived for these options. But it was six months after
the first options were issued that someone circulated the right
rumour: You have to hold the stock three years to qualify for
long-term capital gains.

The tax question wasn't actually that important to me
because my plan was to give away about 80% of whatever I made from the options to tax-deductible organiza-
tions anyway; so I would only have to pay tax on the 20%
I kept. This was a stringent requirement of the Great
Rationalization.

There was a second legal detail it took me a while to find
out about. When Cort made his offer of a stock option at $37,
the stock was already substantially higher. Several weeks after
I started work I received the actual papers and saw that they
had been back-dated to August 1, when the stock was indeed
selling at $37. That made me nervous, though Cort said it was
okay. I could hardly argue, I rationalized, not knowing the
law, not wishing to seem ungrateful or disrespectful, and – of
course – not wishing to delay or devalue my options. Certain
kinds of back-dating options are against The Rules. Yet it is
very tempting for a company whose stock is in the midst of an
explosion to borrow a couple of weeks from the past greatly to
increase a new employee's incentive. Should I have quit when
I found out? Should I have put on my plastic handcuffs and
marched over to the S.E.C. to check? Or was this one of
those rules everybody cheats on a little? (For example, around
the same time I learned from a classmate that his employer,
a highly reputable major publishing company, gives its
employees substantial weekly expense accounts, knowing full
well that most of the money is not used for business expenses,
but as *untaxed* salary instead.)

I think I was like a person entering a steambath for the
first time. It seemed dangerously hot – but then I knew it was
supposed to be hot. If things were hotter than normal, one of

the regular bathers in there with me would surely turn down the steam before anyone keeled over.

Most of the secretaries had options, too, though they didn't seem to care. We had terrific secretaries with mediocre secretarial skills. Binkie was assigned to me when I arrived, but sat about a block away working for one of the generals. After two months I summoned the courage to invite her to Cambridge for the Yale game. As we neared Harvard stadium we were given colourful fliers, which turned out to be our own 'multi-savings envelopes' handed out by what must have been our own campus representative. He had decided this would be the fastest way to get rid of 10,000 fliers. However, since revelling football fans are not big on mail-order offers right before a game, Binkie and I walked to the stadium on a carpet of multi-savings envelopes. I wondered whether there would be enough sales to pay for printing all those envelopes and who would rake them all up after the game. It was one of those boring games, I should add in fairness to the Yalies, where Harvard was hopelessly outclassed and disgusted alumni were abandoning their $50 scalped seats midway through the fourth quarter. With forty-two seconds to go, the elated fans from New Haven were waving their handkerchiefs in a blizzard of mock surrender and shouting about how they were No. 1. Harvard proceeded to score sixteen points and earn the *Crimson* headline, which I hung in my office, 'Harvard Beats Yale, 29–29.'

A few weeks later Binkie and her boss left NSMC. With Binkie gone, I managed to steal Maggie from the receptionist's deck, and she stayed with me from then on. Maggie was the youngest girl in the office; I was the youngest young entrepreneur. I was even younger than the mailboy. Maggie and I both had been well sheltered by our families. Maggie's parents still forbade her taking cabs home from work late at night, so suspicious were they of cab drivers' intentions. My parents still forbade my 'using' No Doz tablets to stay awake late at night, placing this Bristol-Myers 'drug' in the same category as heroin. We both felt shelter from the big bad world was unnecessary – everyone around us and we ourselves were fast becoming rich, rich, rich.

Among the people NSMC made richest was Jack Frankel, our business-card printer. Between changing faces and changing titles, we probably used as many cards as IBM. My first set read, 'Director of Campus Businesses.' In my twenty months with NSMC I was given six different sets as we careened through eight major reorganizations, each with its own organization chart. The reorganizations were necessary to keep pace with the company's remarkable growth. We began referring to the lines and boxes that represented our corporate structure as the *'charte du jour.'*

Each chart was more sophisticated than the last. As you know, organization charts are generally pyramid-shaped. I noticed some odd things at the base of the pyramid, but failed to notice two odd things at the top – where odd things have farther-reaching consequences. First, as with most companies, the chief executive officer (Cort, who for a while was also the chief operating officer) reported to the Board of Directors (elected by the shareholders). However, being by far the largest shareholder, Cort could pretty well elect whomever he pleased to the Board. And all but two of the Board members reported to Cort somewhere else on the chart. They were his generals or subsidiary presidents, whom he had turned to gold and who were unlikely to make too many criticisms.

One of the two who did not report to Cort elsewhere on the chart was the Chairman of the Board, his father, Cortes G. Randell, a distinguished international-business consultant. The other was Dr Frank G. Dickey, Executive Director of the National Commission on Accrediting, who had agreed to serve on the Board as a favour to his friend, Mr Randell, Senior. Cort would let you draw your own conclusions as he explained how this was the organization responsible for granting or withholding a university's accreditation, which was, of course, vital to its existence. To be sure, anyone who thought about it would probably decide that a man like this would never dream of using his influence to secure special advantages for a private company, that a man like this probably knew little about business in general and less still about a particular business whose Board meetings he might occasionally attend. But if anyone is like me, he sometimes prefers to fantasize than to think critically in the middle of a good story. Speaking of fantasy, one of the many executives who had never seen, spoken with by phone, or corresponded with the alleged Dr Dickey suggested that no such man or National Commission actually existed. Fantastic! The idea had never even *occurred* to me, but now that it was suggested it had the ring of fundamental truth. (By the time of this suggestion, I had become quite cynical about the party line.) I decided to do a little research and confess I was a little disappointed to find confirmation of his existence. A man fitting the right description was listed under the Graduate School of Education in the *Harvard Alumni Directory.*

Unlike many public companies, NSMC had no outside bankers or investment people helping to direct company affairs. Like most public companies, the Board had to trust the ability and judgement of the chief executive officer, since you can't rule by committee an hour a month. Only when the growth curve begins to slump does a board usually take a close look and consider changing commanders-in-chief. One of my professors at the Harvard Business School, who happens to be a Director of the Pennsylvania Company (sister of the railroad), holds the view that the job of 'Director' needs a major overhauling. As an increasing number of stockholder suits are being brought against directors, directors are beginning to agree. You can't fault Dr Dickey for his lack of involvement with NSMC. He was probably as involved as most 'honorary' directors are with their companies. The role of Director, as generally conceived, required no more. However, my professor sees a new conception of this role, under which directors would take their responsibilities more seriously. Directors, he thinks, will have full-time staff employees to keep them properly informed and to conduct the necessary investigations.

Anyway, Cort reported to people he elected, who reported to him. That was point one. The second odd point appeared when the post of chief operating officer was split from that of chief executive officer. As usual, the chief operating officer (Roger Walther) reported to the chief executive officer (Cort), who spent most of his time on long-range planning, financing, and acquisitions. Not usual was the way the controller – twenty-seven-year-old John Stalick, author of a Pashto-English dictionary – reported to the chief executive officer instead of to the chief operating officer. Instead of Roger's finding out how his operations were doing and then presenting this information to Cort, he had to go to Cort to find out how things were going. One might almost have thought there were things Cort didn't want Roger to know about.

After the three weeks I was Director of Campus Businesses, we changed me to Director of Market Research and Development, then to Director of Program Planning, then to Vice-President of Market Development, then to Vice-President of New Ventures, along with a special set of cards for President of University Products Corp. Note that I was getting no closer to the top. The bottom was growing under me as NSMC grew from 200 to 2,000 employees. And throughout all the title changes and reorganizations I was doing essentially the same job: Reviewing scads of ideas for new projects brought to NSMC and trying to get a few of the few good ones off the ground.

Was I qualified for this job? Well, I had my strong points and my weak points. I was smart and hard-working. But I lacked experience and was not a born judge of people. At the time I had to make do with the following perception of human nature. I had decided that there were at least two kinds of people. The first is the man who watches a situation comedy on TV and makes it funnier by turning up the volume of the canned laughter. The second is the man who is packing up for a two-week trip to Aspen. He puts out the garbage, shuts off the heat, turns out the light (the blaring stereo will shut itself off when the record is over), locks both doors, leaves a note for the postman, has a great vacation, and returns to, 'homa, where the wind comes sweeping down the plxzxhoma, where the wind comes sweeping down the plxzxhoma, where the wind comes sweeping down the plxzxhoma, where the wind comes sweeping down the . . .' Sometimes this insight was helpful; sometimes it was hard to apply.

Up the hall, Tan and Ed were busily overseeing the distribution of hundreds of thousands of CompuJob résumé forms and the sale of their service to Big Business. An efficient public-relations campaign brought NSMC and CompuJob some glowing publicity. The concept of computerized job placement was exciting, as was the story of rich young entrepreneurs. Unfortunately, in expanding from one campus to 2,000, the program lost a pile of money. At that point, Tan and Ed, with NSMC stock – not options – then valued at about $1 million each, I believe, left NSMC to develop a resort hotel in Nassau.

By this time I had a boss and I was well along with a number of projects. Foremost was my interest in Foosball, a table soccer game two or four can play, highly popular throughout Europe. (While fellow Let's Go editors spent their time abroad trudging around museums and monuments, I fed pfennigs into Foosball and pinball machines.) Invest a quarter and play ten balls. There was only one company seriously involved with the game in the U.S., and the college market was virtually untouched. I told Cort late one night we should consider importing fifty such games as a test.

Usually by ten or eleven at night there were only a few of us left in the office and this was when I generally got a chance to talk to Cort. His shirttail would be hanging out of his baggy pants and he seemed more human than in the middle of an overambitious schedule of formal meetings with outsiders. Despite gaping yawns that did little to beautify his football-fullback features, you knew the numbers and plans and pending deals were still buzzing in his head. He was never detached or contemplative. He was living NSMC. He had an immediate answer or order for everything. Trying to run his company single-handedly long after it was too large for one man to manage effectively, Cort was forever ignoring lines of authority, frequently countermanding orders, often authorizing the impossible, and occasionally contradicting his own instructions. However, he rarely sounded dictatorial or angry. The strength of his orders came from his enthusiasm, his professed faith in you, his not giving you time to argue, and the impressive figure he cut – both financially and physically.

At six-foot-three, 220 pounds, Cort was, appropriately, the biggest man in the company. He needed constant fuel injections to keep going, eating several nonmeals a day. A medical problem prevented his eating much at a time, so he ate frequently instead. Nonmeals ranged from a hot dog and a Sprite at the airport to a cottage-cheese fruit salad plate sent up to the office to a half-eaten filet mignon at the Four Seasons.

He didn't drink much, was always formal in the presence of young ladies, and would not play cards for money. He usually spent three or four days a week in New York (he had a suite at the Americana, and when we moved to Park Avenue offices, at the Waldorf) and was home in Maclean, Virginia, outside Washington, on weekends. Home was a modest $600,000 castle, complete with dungeon, facing the Potomac, on which Cort navigated his hydrofoil, his fleet of radio-controlled model boats, and a fifty-five-foot yacht that slept twelve. He would often spend Saturday mornings in the top-floor Washington office, where all the accounting functions were performed. Sundays he would entertain merger candidates on the yacht.

Cort was always complimentary to me, expected me to do great things, and was, I think, genuinely warm. Despite the wildness of some of his projections and expectations, his deaf ear to the practical business problems we faced in trying to make his dreams come true, I wanted nothing more than to justify his faith in me. Cort did the math and decided we should either import 5,000 Foosball games or acquire the one company already in the Foosball business.

It seemed to me a lot safer to acquire an already profitable company than to import 5,000 games, so I got my air-travel card and my youth-fare card and flew to Cincinnati. For some reason the President of the Foosball concern was cold to the prospect of acquisition negotiations with a twenty-one-year-old (his first tactful question as I walked in was an alarmed, 'How *old* are you?'), but I assumed my winningest whiz-kid expression and somehow managed to persuade him to come to New York to meet Mr Randell.

The night before Mr Foosball was scheduled to arrive, Cort, a few generals, and I held a prenegotiation strategy meeting at which it was decided to offer up to $500,000 in stock, but no more because several disadvantages of the company, such as the tarnished image of the coin-operated – machine industry, made it 'not worth reaching for.' So Cort's first offer to Mr Foosball was $1 million. This was my introduction to one of Cort's most important strategies. As his assistant put it, 'Cort loses all the battles, but is winning the war.' Cort never had the patience really to negotiate; his growth timetable wouldn't allow it. He also preferred to be thought of as a nice guy, than as a selfish, tough businessman. I realized how lucky I was to have been hired by Cort and not by one of his more businesslike generals when I discovered I had a higher salary than my boss and six times the stock option.

CHAPTER FIVE

Funny Money

The ruble is officially equal to $1.11.
On the black market, tourists can
easily get three rubles for $1, but penalties
for being caught are severe.
*Let's Go II, The Student Guide To
Adventure*

Yap islanders . . . use special kinds of
stones as money. . . . Some of them are
too large to move, but everyone knows
who owns them.
Money and Credit: Impact and Control
JAMES S. DUESENBERRY

If the Bank runs out of Money, it may
issue as much Money of its own as it
may need by merely writing on any
ordinary paper.
The Rules of Monopoly
PARKER BROTHERS, INC

Luckily, we squelched the Foosball deal. Our investment
banker straightened it out somehow with their investment
banker. The Foosball people changed their name to American
Youth Marketing Corporation and started thinking about a
public offering. I added one wholesale Foosball game to my
private gamut of gimmicks.

That was not the only acquisition I attempted to arrange. In my early days at the company we were all encouraged to be on the lookout for possible acquisitions, and were promised finder's fees for those that were consummated. I don't remember the exact terms, but Cort told me I would get so many shares for firms with such and such earnings, so many for larger firms, and so many more for still larger firms. Employees began spending so much energy coming up with outrageous companies to acquire that the finder's fees were eventually discontinued.

I visited a notebook manufacturer to sell them on inserting some of our fliers in their notebooks, but before I knew it we were talking about acquisitions and mergers and synergy. I walked around the plant with the Owner-President and tried to look for whatever you look for when you walk around somebody's plant. It seemed pretty neat, but did that mean they were efficient or that they weren't busy? There were offensive buzzers to signal the beginning and end of the half-hour lunch break, but did that mean the labour force was well under control or that morale was lousy and a strike was imminent? The plant was attractive and modern on the outside, but did that mean the company was prosperous and planning for the future or that the company was burdened with excessive, nonproductive overheads that were choking it to death? The President told me they had their own truck for deliveries to the middle-Atlantic states, which seemed a smart economy move to me. Then he told me he had discovered the driver had been siphoning off tons of notebooks and they were discontinuing the truck, which seemed a smart economy move to me. I figured that as long as I kept quiet and looked wise, the President would not guess I had never seen a paper-converting plant before — would not guess that the last time I had visited a factory was on our fourth-grade trip to the Wonder Bread company.

I knew enough to ask the President what his sales and earnings were (how else could I calculate my finder's fee?). He explained that his company had lost a few hundred thousand dollars recently but was beginning to turn around.

Thus I learned the meaning of 'a turnaround situation.' He said that all he would ask for his company would be a sum equal to the value of his losses. Behind my poker face, my brain, into all of this over its head, was trying to figure out how a *loss* would have value. Why wouldn't he base his asking price on something a little more cheerful, like profit projections? (You can see how my analysis was biased by my enrolment in the NSMC School of Optimistic Financial Management.) On the way home I put the pieces together. As far as earnings were concerned, I saw that if this company were now breaking even it would not hurt NSMC to combine its earnings with theirs. As far as taxes were concerned, NSMC could deduct this company's prior years' losses from NSMC profits this year, and pay less taxes this year. Thus I learned, in something less than accurate form, what was meant by the 'value of a tax loss carry forward.' We didn't buy it.

Then there was the company in the Southwest which we can call the Alpha Company, the way Harvard Business School does when it wants to talk about a company without getting anyone in trouble. Again, I was there to sell the President something, but he was out in the factory when I arrived, so I was entertained by the General Manager. Who proceeded to tell me in confidence what a tyrant the President was, how everyone hated him, how he wished we would buy the company (I was just there on a sales call, but obligingly switched missions on the spot), how all we would have to do then would be to fire the President and make him, the faithful General Manager, President, and watch the money roll in. To document all this he showed me internal memoranda, pro formas (budgets for future operations, I learned), and his own résumé. He promised to sit in on my meeting with the paranoiac, megalomaniacal President, steer the conversation to acquisition, and let me know afterwards how much of what the President said was truth, and how much, trimming. He frequently checked to see that his intercom was shut off; he gave me a code name to use if I ever wanted to call him in the office and his home phone if I ever wanted to call him at night.

The President was not as bad a character as the General Manager had led me to expect, nor even, perhaps, as bad a character as the General Manager. Nonetheless, astute observer of human relations that I am, I concluded that Alpha had a management problem. (I was surprised to learn, two or three years after my contact with Alpha, that these two men were still working together. I don't know how they do it.)

Although my early acquisition sorties were all abortive, plenty of other wild acquisitions did go through, which accounted for the phenomenal growth of NSMC sales and stock price. During my twenty months at NSMC sales grew from $3 million to nearly $100 million, and the stock, which had been issued at $6, reached a high of $143! One article on the company bulletin board confirmed that our stock had grown faster than any other in 1968. Our company name was synonymous with success, prosperity, and a brilliant future. The investment community had fallen madly in love with us.

NSMC by no means lacked competition on the Old Acquisition Trail. The pioneer conglomerators had spotted a golden frontier. In the two years between my leaving college and entering business school, 10,000 acquisitions were completed. NSMC laid twenty-two of the claims. Dolly Madison – once just an ice-cream concern – staked out thirty-five.

A word of explanation must accompany the charts of NSMC growth that follow. When you account for 'pooling of interests' mergers, you are required to 'restate' past years' figures as though the new companies you have acquired had always been part of your company. This is done to allow a meaningful comparison with past years, and on the theory that when you merge with a company you merge with its past history as well.

This method of accounting does not make for dramatic comparisons, but is only required in audited financial statements. What a company shows in its press kit or in the 'Financial Highlights' section of its annual report is another story. The chart of NSMC sales growth, for example, shows a jump of more than 500% between 1968 and 1969. However, on a 'fully adjusted basis' the jump would have been

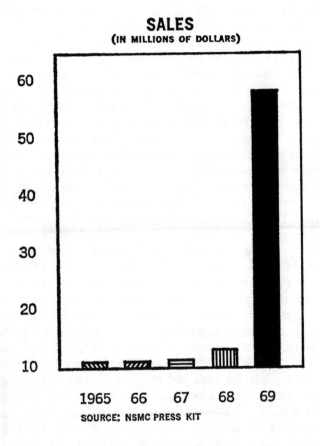

SALES
(IN MILLIONS OF DOLLARS)

SOURCE: NSMC PRESS KIT

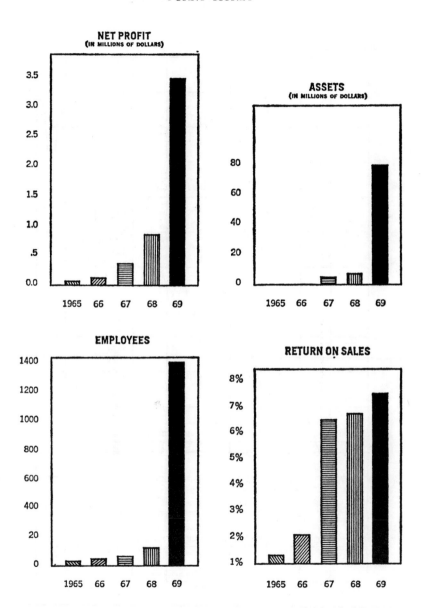

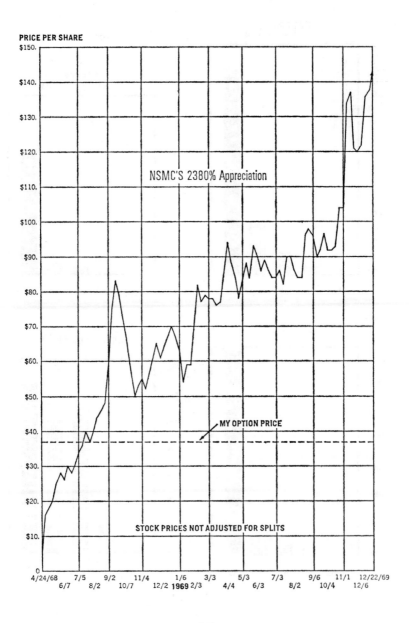

PRICE PER SHARE

NSMC'S 2380% Appreciation

MY OPTION PRICE

STOCK PRICES NOT ADJUSTED FOR SPLITS

more like 30%. And then we are still left to wonder how much of this increase was attributable to companies acquired by the 'purchase' (rather than 'pooling') method, which does not require a combination of past financial histories.

Manhattan's population is two million; the Bronx has a population of 1.5 million. If Manhattan's boundaries were extended to include the Bronx, would you get all excited by the massive influx of immigrants to Manhattan? Or would you begin to think of Manhattan, as redefined, as having had a population of 3.5 million for quite some time? Is Manhattan any more crowded? Some Wall Street analysts apparently thought so.

Many companies seemed to have decided it was easier and faster to buy someone else's profits, or profit projections, than to generate them internally. Wall Street appeared to approve, as almost every acquisition rumour was rewarded with a substantial jump in the market value of the acquisitor's stock – making it that much easier for the acquisitor to afford the acquisition.

Randell's often-announced plan was to triple sales and earnings each year. He would quickly rattle off the sales for the years 1965 through 1968 – $215,000, $573,000, $1.8 million, $5.5 million – and then sort of grinningly apologize for 1969, when they went a little faster than usual to $67 million. People rarely interrupted to ask how long that could keep up; by 1975 NSMC would be the largest corporation in the world. You don't lightly interrupt a high-powered multimillionaire who clearly does not like to be interrupted – *particularly if you want him to touch you and turn you to gold.* Virtually all the prospective investors and merger candidates had just that natural desire. They *wanted* to believe. It was that it was, and that was that, so to speak. I suspect faith is almost as important to business as it is to religion.

Thus when Cort announced earnings would triple, investors scrambled for the stock, and it went up. Investors, I learned, are more interested in what earnings *will* be than in what they are. At the time it was not uncommon for exciting companies

57

(glamour stocks) to sell for thirty or thirty-five times their *estimated earnings;* NSMC stock sold for something like 100 times the previous year's earnings.

For those of you who know even less than I about the mechanics of the stock market, I have provided a short, do-it-yourself course for the construction of a $100-million enterprise.

Look at it this way. How much would you pay to own a wallet that somehow produced a dollar a year? $3? That would be a good deal, since after three years you would have your $3 back, and thereafter you would be getting a free dollar for ever and ever. The going rate for such wallets seems to be about $20. If you give a savings bank $20, they will give you $1 (5%) every year for ever and ever. Drawing the $20 out of the bank stops the flow of dollars; you have sold the wallet to someone else for $20 and now he is getting those dollars for ever and ever.

Now how much would you pay for a wallet that leads you to believe, with no guarantees, that it just might be able to produce $3 instead of $1 in the second year and maybe $9 the third year and perhaps a little more each year thereafter? That's more or less what NSMC was asking Wall Street, and they answered, '$100, which is 100 times what you're earning now, but only thirty-three times what you might earn next year, and perhaps only eleven times what you could earn the year after . . .'

There are a lot of different wallets – stocks – on the market, and each one has its own story. Whether a stock is valued at three times or twenty times or 100 times its earnings (profits) depends on such factors as: Are the earnings in the future likely to decrease, stay where they are, or increase? How risky is the business of this company – might its optimistic projections turn sour? What portion of the profits will actually be mailed to me as a dividend, and what portion will the directors we have elected vote to reinvest in the company ('retained earnings')?

Deciding what value a stock should have is the business of highly paid members of the investment community. It is their job to decide whether a company really can produce what it thinks it can, how much risk is involved, and so on. Since this 'decision' is not made by a committee or a judge, but by the laws of supply and demand in the market, they also have to be mass psychologists: They have to figure out what their neighbours up and down the Street are going to do, and do it first. If they think more of their neighbours are going to be buying some stock than selling it, they want to buy it first, because when there are more buyers than sellers for something, its price goes up. (And vice versa.)

In order to figure out what a stock 'should' be selling for, Wall Street firms send analysts like my roommate Humphrey to visit companies, hear their stories, ask critical questions, and then decide what their earnings are most likely to be in the future. Then they look at the past performance of the price of the company's stock in relation to its earnings. If a stock has generally sold for twelve times earnings ($12 for a wallet producing $1 a year), then it is likely that the mass of buyers and sellers who make up 'the market' will continue to value the stock of this company at about twelve times its earnings, unless there is a change in the company's rate of growth or the risk of its ventures or something. So if Humphrey comes back thinking that next year's earnings will be $1.25, we can figure the stock 'should' sell for about 12 x $1.25, or $15. If it is now selling for less than $15, perhaps we should buy it!

This relationship of a stock's price to its earnings, called either 'price-earnings ratio' or 'multiple,' is very important. NSMC had a multiple of about thirty-five times estimated earnings, or 100 times actual earnings. General Motors and like companies sell for about ten times earnings because they are too big to grow very fast; because manufacturers can't grow as fast as 'service companies', because next year's earnings are likely to be about the same as this year's. The old idea that one dollar is no better or worse than another doesn't hold when investors are looking at the earnings of companies. A dollar of earnings in a glamour company may be valued more highly than a dollar of earnings in an old, uninteresting company because of the better growth prospects of the glamour company.

Since Randell couldn't get his *own* company to triple its earnings each year, he used NSMC stock that Wall Street was valuing at 100 times earnings to buy other companies for, say, thirty times earnings. Like an American on a fourteen-day excursion to Spain living luxuriously on $10 a day, the exchange rate was in his favour. I gathered that this was what people meant by 'leverage.' I learned that high-multiple stock used to purchase other companies or raise capital was called 'funny money.'

Cort and his assistants constantly updated their shopping list of companies, as they called it, and spent virtually full time making acquisitions. The larger NSMC grew, the larger the chunks they were able to buy up – and the larger they *had* to be to make an appreciable dent. At first, they courted companies with sales well under $1 million; a year later, companies generally had to have sales in excess of $5 million to be considered.

Whereas for most companies, especially before merger fever began a few years ago, an acquisition was a major event requiring perhaps one or two years to consummate, NSMC had joined the Acquisition-a-Month Club. Cort put the procedure on an assembly line. He had the lengthy legal documents of acquisition recorded on the company's IBM Magnetic Tape Selectric Typewriter (MT/ST – like a player piano), with blanks that would be filled in for the company name, number of shares of stock, and other particulars. Press the button, fill in the blanks, sign here, here, here, and here, and you've got a deal.

The standard NSMC presentation to potential subsidiaries – fifteen NSMC executives around the conference table helping Cort tell the story – became so frequent and burdensome that someone suggested it be filmed. That way, several presentations could be made at once with no tie-up of NSMC manpower. We could see the day when Cort would choose companies from the Standard and Poor's Directory and let his team of projectionists and MT/ST operators handle the details. No skilled negotiators would be necessary, since at 100 times earnings Cort could easily afford to offer an across-the-board, irresistible thirty times earnings for the companies he wanted.

To see just how this works, let's go through an actual, typical NSMC acquisition. The Colad company in Buffalo, New York, has been making book covers and related products for about twenty-five years. When NSMC broached the subject of acquisition, Colad had gradually built up to sales of about $2.5 million and earnings of about $100,000. Colad's President had built the company from nothing. He probably knew that when they were bought or sold, solid but unexciting manufacturing companies like his were generally valued at around ten times earnings – which in his case would be $1 million. Not a bad retirement fund.

Cort wanted to buy Colad and gave its President (who owned nearly 100% of the stock; it was a private, not a public, company) the full royal treatment. He probably got to fly in *Snoopy,* Cort's $700,000 Lear Jet, complete with full-time pilot and co-pilot, Dewey and Tex. He met with the fifteen NSMC executives around the $2,000 conference table in the Time-Life Building and heard about all the exciting projects and youth-market media that were in the works. After the meeting he was led upstairs for dinner at the Tower Suite, *prix fixe* at $11.50, plus drinks, tax, and tip, where after a couple of courses he was given a 'touch of pomegranate sherbet to refresh his appetite before the main course.' (Naturally, he painted a rather proud and optimistic picture of Colad's prospects and gave Cort a royal treatment of his own. He probably did not stress that book covers seem to be on the way out – kids don't use them as much as they used to – or other problems.)

He thought about NSMC's twenty-two highly paid account executives (salesmen) selling national advertising on the inside of his book covers (like advertising on the inside of air-sickness bags? But Cort said it would be an effective medium, and Cort was a marketing genius); he thought about becoming a director of a company soon to be listed on the

New York Stock Exchange; he thought about working with a lot of creative, enthusiastic young people; he thought about giving up ownership and control of his life's work; he thought about getting out from under many of his business worries and problems; he thought about the $3 million(!) Cort had offered. He told us fifteen NSMC executives that he had tremendous respect for what we were helping Cort to do. He told us that he was still young at heart – and proceeded to do twenty excellent push-ups in front of us. And then a few days later the merger was announced.

To illustrate the math, let me simplify the facts without changing the theory. Let's say that without Colad, NSMC has earnings of $100,000 and that the ownership of NSMC is divided into 100,000 shares. Thus, NSMC's earnings per share are $1 – each share is like a wallet that had produced a dollar, though this money is retained to be reinvested in the company. Since Wall Street is valuing NSMC stock at 100 times current earnings, each share sells for $100.

Now, in order to pay the President of Colad $3 million for his company, NSMC has to use 30,000 shares of stock (at $100 each = $3 million). The people who own the existing 100,000 shares of NSMC stock are asked whether they would be willing to see their company divided into even smaller pieces – 130,000 pieces instead of 100,000 which means that everyone will have a smaller piece of the pie. But they say yes, because they know the pie will be bigger. More technically, they know that their equity (ownership) in the company will be diluted by a smaller percentage than the percentage by which the earnings of the company will be increased – *earnings per share* will increase.

So now NSMC is divided into 130,000 shares; but there are earnings of $200,000 – NSMC's plus Colad's – which divides out to $1.54 of earnings per share. Many investors assume that NSMC will continue to sell at 100 times current earnings, so they figure the stock is a steal at $100. They buy it, which makes it go up until it reaches about $154.

NSMC shareholders are delighted to see their shares increased in value. The President of Colad is delighted because his 30,000 shares are now worth about $4.5 million.[1] The people who bought the stock between $100 and $153 have already made a nice gain. And the people who bought it at $154 are eagerly awaiting future events which they hope will work out just as well.

Note that in all this getting rich everyone is doing, nothing tangible has been added to the economy – no book covers that would not otherwise have been made, no new profits, nothing. The gimmick, of course, is that NSMC should no longer sell at 100 times earnings because it is now partly an unglamorous, slowly growing book-cover company. Perhaps the stock 'should' really stay at $100, despite earnings of $1.54 a share – which would work out to a multiple of 'only' sixty-five. This did not happen for two reasons: (a) NSMC tried to convince everyone they could turn Colad into a fast-growing, exciting company and realize synergy; (b) fads are not always awfully analytical – enthusiasm (greed?) over reason.

You've passed the course.

Randell's earnings prophecies were self-fulfilling. By announcing phenomenal earnings projections he got a phenomenal valuation of NSMC stock, which then allowed him to buy enough earnings to meet his projections. Then, to keep the momentum high, as all glamour stocks must, he

---

[1] In this particular case, the lucky (shrewd?) President actually received $2 million of the $3 million in cash, and the acquisition was treated as a "purchase" rather than as a "pooling of interests." The difference will be discussed in a later chapter. Because most of NSMC's acquisitions were accounted for as poolings of interest. I have, for the purposes of this illustration, pretended that Colad was handled that way also.

When NSMC had to pay cash for a company, as in this case, it would sell unregistered stock to some third party, such as the Harvard Endowment Fund, at a bargain price - say 25% under the open-market price - to compensate for the fact that unregistered stock could not be sold easily until it was registered, which could take months or years. Such transactions are called "private placements" of "letter stock" at a certain per cent "discount." "Letter stock" is synonymous with "unregistered stock" and refers to the letter that must accompany the stock attesting to its purchase as a long-term *investment*. Sometimes it is called "investment letter stock."

would make another round of phenomenal projections. As long as he bought companies for a lower multiple of their earnings than the multiple at which NSMC stock was valued, earnings would increase more than equity would be diluted – so earnings per share would increase. As with a chain letter, investors and acquired companies don't get hurt as long as the snowball keeps growing exponentially forever: Impossible, but enticing if you're one of the first to sign up. Chain letters are illegal.

Also like a chain letter, NSMC's growth depended on confidence in the chain. If people fear the chain may be broken or that there is something shady going on, they will not participate and it will collapse. Randell managed to build an unparalleled mutual admiration society that could allay almost any fears. The auditors probably figured that if something disreputable were going on, then White and Case, one of the largest law firms in the world, would not sit quietly as NSMC's counsel. White and Case was probably reassured by the fact that Peat, Marwick, Mitchell apparently had no qualms about the financial statements. Morgan Guaranty and Donaldson, Lufkin, & Jenrette, when they took their substantial positions in the stock, were probably pleased that the Harvard Endowment Fund had already taken a position, while Harvard probably was pleased about the growing ranks of Harvard MBAs in the company, including two who assisted Cort full time. The MBAs may have heard about NSMC through favourable articles in *Business Week* and *Ad Age*. And everyone wanted a ride in Cort's Lear Jet. (I flew with him from Las Vegas to New York; but that was before he installed the telephone. . . .) When you are in such good company, you don't try too hard to find holes in the story. You take a lot for granted.

I remember a psychology experiment we studied in college. Five students were hired as subjects for a 'perception test.' The first four to arrive were told how to behave and seated in a row in front of a movie screen. The last student to arrive was given no instructions and was seated at the end of the row. Two squares were projected onto the screen and the students were asked which was bigger. They were told to answer in order, from left to right, which meant the unsuspecting fifth student would always be the last to answer. Each student in turn said that, obviously, the left square was bigger. Then six shades of red were projected – which was darkest? The third, each said in turn. Some hand-drawn circles – which most nearly round? Although it was fairly close, each of the five decided the first circle was most nearly perfect. Then four lines – which was longest? The fourth line was longest; however, the first four students, by instruction, chose the second line. What do you think the fifth student said?

Perhaps after reading how Cort bought nearly $100 million worth of other companies' sales with funny money, you are tempted, as I was, to write a letter to the editor like one that appeared in *Business Week* in a 1970 issue. The letter said that if a price-earnings ceiling were placed on stocks, 'stocks would not be overinflated, the financial community would not be in a mess' and funny money would be taken out of circulation. If all stocks were sold at ten times their earnings, the letter said, 'price swings would not be severe, and people would not lose much of their savings and their jobs,' and if 'earnings increased, the price of the stock would increase by the same proportion.'

Upon reflection, though, there are at least two flaws in this neat solution. First, everyone would want to buy the stock of a company that expected to show healthy earnings growth each year – and almost no one would want to sell it. There would not be enough to go around. How would you ration IBM stock, for example, which sells at around fifty times earnings because it grows about 20% a year? Second, the stock market is a key mechanism by which the nation, consciously or unconsciously, allocates its capital resources.[1] People invested tremendous sums in a company called Recognition Equipment for years before it made a profit at all, because they

---

[1] There is evidence that Wall Street is less "key" in this respect than they might have you believe. "Equity issues supply less than 5% of the new capital needed to finance business." (*Business Week*, Oct. 31, 1970.)

thought machines that could read numbers and characters (on cheques, for example) would be tremendously important to data processing in future decades. The stock was selling at an infinite multiple, since there were no earnings; but finally the bugs were ironed out of the machines and investors' hopes were largely realized. How would you finance speculative ventures if not through speculative stock issues?

True, many new ideas will fail and the capital invested will be lost. However, the S.E.C. attempts to force companies to make it very clear to investors just how much risk is involved in their investment. In order to satisfy the S.E.C., many prospectuses for new issues have to make comments like this:

> Because what we are trying to do has never been done before and we are not very well qualified to do it or positive that people will care even if we can, there is absolutely no assurance that we will ever make a profit.

Until recently, this kind of statement only served to whet the excitement of speculators, like me, who saw what Omega Equities had done (25c to $25) and weren't going to let the S.E.C. or other conservative Depression-raised types keep them from cashing in.

I reasoned this way: Although similar to horse races or roulette, the market does have three slight redeeming qualities. First, in a casino you have less than a 50% chance of winning, while in the market as a whole the average investment should grow with the American economy, which some people feel will grow, despite minor setbacks, forever. Second, when you invest in Wall Street, your capital is generally allocated to projects you might consider more worthwhile than the pockets of other gamblers and casino owners. Third, people who play the market are probably better able to sustain losses than some of the people hooked on the horses.

Perhaps this is how the people reasoned who read the Class Student Services prospectus and decided to buy some. Although delayed, the stock was indeed coming out at $15 a share, as

Dan Richard had promised, and I had passed up the opportunity to own 3,000 shares in favour of owning NSMC stock options likely to be worth considerably more. Still, you can imagine that I read the Class prospectus with considerable interest:

> The securities offered by this Prospectus are highly speculative. In analyzing this offering, investors should carefully consider the following:
>
> (1) Due to the nature of the Company's business, it makes large cash outlays for production and preparation for its sales and marketing programs, without any assurance as to the amounts of revenues, if any, it will receive or as to when such revenues will be received.
>
> (2) The Company has not operated profitably since its organization on May 9, 1968. From that date, through December 31, 1968, the Company was in its developmental stage and sustained losses of $297,394.09 or an average of $45,752 per month. . . .
>
> The Company commenced sales operations in September, 1968. Since then it has done business on a limited scale only. Through December 31, 1968, its sales were nominal, amounting to $68,332.29. These revenues were derived from sales of advertising, sales of the Company's own products, and sales of other companies' products . . . and were derived in a four-month period immediately following distribution of the CLASS Guide . . . [Evidently, mail-order sales had not measured up to the $1 per each of the million and a half guides distributed, as hoped.]
>
> . . . There can be no assurance that operational revenues will increase sufficiently to substantially offset reduction of the Company's working capital. Accordingly, additional financing may be required in the future. There can be no assurance that additional financing will be available if required, or as to the terms of such financing, if available.

(3) The company is presently not in any position to pay dividends and does not intend to do so. There can be no assurance that dividends will ever be declared.

(4) Prior to this offering there was no public market for the Common Stock of the Company, and the offering price ($15.00) of the shares offered hereby was arbitrarily determined by negotiation with the Representative of the Underwriters [Pressman, Frolich & Frost, Inc.]. Such offering price has no relationship to the present book value of the Company's outstanding shares (approximately $0.19 per share), nor to past earnings, since the company has only recently commenced operation and has no earnings to date . . .

(5) The Company through this offering is seeking to raise capital to continue and expand its present operations and develop new activities. There can be no assurance that proceeds of this offering will be adequate for these purposes or that the Company's projects will be profitable. . . .

There were ten more paragraphs of like nature in this section of the prospectus cautioning prospective investors, and others peppered throughout. As you might expect, investors quickly bought the stock that was being offered. Within a few months the price had risen from $15 to $30 a share. My 3,000 shares would have been worth $90,000 (they would have been un-registered, and thus hard to sell); but I was not complaining.

With twelve months left to go before I could exercise my NSMC stock options, they were worth $250,000. I started thinking about buying an island off the coast of Northern Maine. ($5,000.) I discovered it by responding to a classified ad in the Harvard *Crimson*, which I had mailed to me every day to keep in touch with the youth market. The headline of the ad was: 'Land In Maine.' First line: 'And stay there.' Well, I had spent eight summers as a camper in Maine and melted at the thought of owning an island up there. 'Why yes, this *is* a lovely cocktail party; you'll have to come up to Maine to see my island sometime.' I think I would have named it Ego Island. What kind of island can one buy for $5,000? The one I had in mind was so far north nothing would grow on it, no one could swim off it. And so far off shore it would be a little risky to sail out to it in anything less than a Coast Guard cutter. Undaunted, I went downstairs to Bankers Trust to investigate the mortgage possibilities. I learned that mortgages are generally written on buildings, not land, and certainly not islands. I learned also that the law on island ownership was a little vague, and that I could not be assured of ownership even with a bill of sale, since the seller might not own it either. I decided against Ego Island largely on the strength of my desire for swimmable water. Instead, I sent off a couple of letters of inquiry to Greek real-estate brokers whose names I had found somewhere. I got back very courteous letters informing me that Greek islands were indeed available, and very swimmable, going for $100,000 and up. Oh, well.

Maggie had only eight months left on her little option and she finally began to believe it might have some value after all ($19,000). Earlier she had offered to trade me her option for a $25-a-week raise – but began to see that she would have been trading $19,000 for $2,500 if I had let her go through with it. Maggie and I frequently had dinner at La Fonda del Sol, a wonderful Spanish restaurant, with wandering musicians, in the lobby of the Time-Life Building. Their mussels, guacamole, tortillas, enchiladas, and mocha parfaits were washed down with a large pitcher of sangría, which eased the pain of the $25 check. Who cares? We were both imminently *nouveaux riches.*

I generally had a sandwich at my desk for lunch unless there were a good business reason to go out. New York lunches ran about $6 a head. Except when my boss occasionally took me to lunch and spent closer to $12. This particular boss (my third in the general shuffle, I think) was a Senior Vice-President, who, with his brother, another V.-P., owned more NSMC stock than anyone else but Cort.

One day he showed me a cashier's cheque for $497,000, which he realized from a private placement of some of his letter stock. His brother sold an equal number of shares at the same time. This was a real, negotiable cheque. Presumably, with a little fuss he could have traded it for 4,970 crisp $100 bills, or 24,850 twenties. Was it conceivable that all these paper profits and numbers I had been mentally manipulating so long might soon become a negotiable reality?

I had become remarkably adept at figuring, cross-figuring, and refiguring my net worth in every conceivable way. Sometimes I would figure the value of my options as though there had been no splits; sometimes I multiplied more shares by lower prices, taking the splits into account. Sometimes I would figure the difference between my option price and the market value of a single share and multiply it by the total number of shares in my option; sometimes I would figure the value a $1 increase in the stock would have on all the shares, and then multiply that by the total number of points by which the market price exceeded my option price. With two splits and three options to deal with (I had been getting more goodies as I went along), there were endless ways to come out to that $250,000. Then I would figure out how much of it to give to whom, and how much the taxes would be on the remainder and what to do with that. Have you ever swum laps? It was very much like swimming in high school when I knew that I had to go seventy-two laps to make a mile and developed endless different ways of counting – forward, backward, in six sets of twelve, twelve sets of six, to thirty-six and back to nought. I believe I had what psychologists call 'an obsession'. When Chet Huntley would say, '. . . leaving the Soviets several options . . .' my mind automatically switched channels.

To avoid gaining weight from all those expensive meals and to avoid the horror and aggravation of the New York subway system, I began walking to and from work. I found that I walked slightly better than a block a minute, so it was about thirty-five minutes each way. I later learned these walks were not so healthy after all, as I breathed in the equivalent of two packs of cigarettes a day. I noticed the fumes, traffic jams, litter and jack-hammers every morning, but had no time to think about ecology or the environment.

Most weekends I worked at least one day, generally both. But every third weekend or so I would fly to Cambridge, rent a car, and degenerate with friends. Between these weekend trips north and business trips to NSMC's Washington office, I became one of Eastern Airlines' best shuttle customers. On New Year's Day, 1970, after taking Maggie home – she lived out on Long Island, even past Kennedy airport – I decided not to go all the way back into the city but rather to La Guardia to wait around for the first flight to Boston. As I stepped bleary-eyed and unsuspecting on to the plane, the Captain said, 'Congratulations, son, you are the first Eastern Airlines' shuttle passenger of the decade.' Shortly thereafter, I received a scroll signed by President Hall of Eastern commemorating my historic flight to Boston. I keep it in the same drawer as you know what.

My other historic flight was in Cort's Lear Jet. *Snoopy* carried five passengers, a bar, and a Lear Jet stereo tapedeck at 600 miles per hour. I had flown many times before at 600 miles per hour, but never two feet from one of the country's most celebrated businessmen in a plane the size and specifications of a fighter jet. Cort was planning to trade up to a ten-passenger jet, complete with private john.

On reflection I decided the most frightening thing about the flight was not how the rain-slicked runway swayed from side to side as we made our landing to refuel in St Louis, but that one might grow accustomed to wild luxuries like this and need them – and even greater luxuries – to be happy. It seems to me that all but the most spiritually content need a gradual improvement in their life-styles to be happy. New toys provide variety, a sense of achievement, status – you name it. But can a $720,000 Lear Jet provide 720 times as much happiness as a fabulous new stereo system? And worse, how much does it cost noticeably to improve your means of transportation when you have a Lear Jet? If you have a Lear Jet at thirty-four, what can you trade up to at forty-four? Worst

71

of all, what if you have to sell the Lear Jet and get back in line at the American Airlines' ticket counter?

It seems to this unqualified philosopher that one can absorb only so much happiness at a time, and that one may as well improve his style of living by the smallest increments that will keep him happy, rather than go all the way for one tremendous orgasm and downhill from there. This will save one money and increase the likelihood of continued improvement. If we have any real hope for widespread happiness among the world's inhabitants, we had better find increments short of Lear Jets and yachts and thirty-acre estates on the Potomac. Even if one acquires the wealth to purchase such luxuries, by legal means within the American business system, can he really use it this way with a clear conscience? I know that many people will argue that he can; Eloy might argue that he can't.

CHAPTER SIX

We Are Hep (Hip?)

> The trend-setting, vocal eighteen- to
> twenty-four-year-old segment of the
> population is impressive now and
> growing extremely fast; they will increase
> their population percentage from today's
> 11% to 25% by 1975[1]
> *You and the Student Market*
> An NSMC sales brochure

Public relations is to selling Wall Street a stock what advertising is to selling the American housewife a soap. NSMC retained a number of different public-relations firms while I was with the company and added a professional ($20,000, plus options) p.r. gal to the corporate staff. The NSMC press kit weighed about two pounds and contained some inspired prose. There are, after all, a number of different ways to tell the same story and we were always anxious to put our best foot forward. Our bottles were never half empty, always half full.

NSMC did not describe itself as a 'poorly managed conglomerate of generally unglamorous companies with moderate

---

[1] "Extremely fast" is an understatement. For this segment of the population to reach 25% by 1973, we would either have to welcome 25 million 18- to 24-year-old immigrants or else wipe out 100 million non-18- to 24-year-old in some kind of disaster. The four-colour lithography of this slick brochure was more impressive than its factual content. Something like a solid-gold garbage truck.

growth rates worth about ten to twenty times earnings'. Instead, Cort conveyed the following two images to support his phenomenal earnings projections and to keep from appearing to be a conglomerate or a chain letter:

I. NSMC WAS IN TOUCH WITH THE YOUTH MARKET, THE EXPERT. THE ORIGINAL NSMC – THE CORE COMPANY – WAS A PROFITABLE GROUP OF EFFECTIVE MEDIA NSMC HAD DEVELOPED TO REACH THIS MARKET.

II. NSMC ADDED TO THE CORE ONLY OUTSTANDING YOUTH-MARKET COMPANIES WHOSE EARNINGS THEIR MARKETING SYSTEM COULD DRAMATICALLY INCREASE. EVEN WITHOUT ADDITIONAL ACQUISITIONS, NSMC EARNINGS WOULD GROW AT A PHENOMENAL RATE.

I think each of these images is worth a chapter. Implicit in both, of course, is the impeccability of everyone involved – Cort and his staff, the lawyers, the accountants, the investment houses, and the others.

First of all, NSMC was in touch with the youth market and was the expert in the field. Put up a shingle and you're a professional. I suspect that Dow Chemical had a better understanding of the youth market than NSMC did.

In a speech to the New York Society of Security Analysts – and what better audience can a public company have – Cort said:

> Our creative people are all under twenty-five. When anyone reaches twenty-five, they're moved into a managerial role – assuming they're qualified, of course. Creativity – which is the premise of marketing – must come from their own peers.

Allusions were frequently made to 'our creative people' as though we had battalions of young creative types dreaming up

74

slogans and campaigns. We did not. All that was done by our clients' ad agencies. There was no personnel procedure by which creative types were moved into management at twenty-five.

Nor did we have weekly readings of student opinion to identify or anticipate trends. Most of the information we had on the youth market came either from a report done for one of our competitors by Marplan in 1966 (have students changed much in four years?) or from *Fortune*'s February 1969 issue on Youth.

Nor could our computer spit out the list of all colleges with such and such characteristics; for example, all schools in the Southwest with at least 50% female enrolment. Like almost everything else, this capability was in the works and might be achieved sometime in the future – but it was discussed as though it already existed. Visionaries have trouble keeping their tenses straight.

Most of our rapidly turned-over management did fall into the twenty-five–thirty-five age group; however, they were too business-oriented to be very student-oriented. Rapidly turned over but never turned on. Because many of the executives were recruited by a Canadian Senior Vice-President (my friend with the $497,000 cheque), including a Canadian Personnel Manager, about half the management group wound up being Canadian. This was another obstacle to their understanding the American youth market. In one of my more rebellious moments against this domination from the North, I ordered and distributed newspapers with the headline: 'Canucks Beg U.S. Protection in Feud with Monaco.' They retaliated by terminating my Canadian lessons at Berlitz.

Of course, being hep (hip?), we all wore suits to work and kept our hair trim – not a beard or moustache on the floor. There was one fellow who sometimes wore a blue blazer and grey slacks and we tried to be tolerant. After a while we hired Steve Nagin, fresh from the editorship of the University of Miami newspaper, and our creative type in residence. Steve's dress varied from suit and tie to tennis sweater and sneakers.

He positioned an antique gumball machine outside his door to supplement his substandard salary and burned incense. I imagine that some of the older and wiser executives mistook the smell for marijuana, but no one complained. I doubt that Steve did much to liberate the rest of the company, or that the rest of the company did much to inhibit him.

Characteristic of NSMC's youthful approach was Tor, the mailboy. A black high school dropout getting his Big Chance? Tor was a sixty-three-year-old with a Ph.D. in sociology from the University of Stockholm, whose gymnastics team had won a gold medal in the 1924 Olympics. Once in a while I would stay at the office all night, using the sample toothpaste, razor blades, shaving cream, and deodorant from one of the million Campus Pacs our subsidiary distributed to students each year. Tor was always the first one to arrive, at around 6.00 a.m., even though he had an hour's subway ride to work and the mail was not delivered until 8.30. It was a challenge for us to communicate as he was hard of hearing and spoke with a heavy accent and I was duller than usual at 6.00 a.m. Tor used to spend most of his free time around our new-ventures area because he enjoyed talking with Maggie (so did everyone else, but Tor had more free time). He also got along famously with Steve Berg, my most successful Program Manager, who got along famously with everyone. Berg, who wore the same pair of red suspenders and, seemingly, smoked the same foul cigar every day for a year, exchanged shouted greetings with Tor whenever he passed by and asked whether Tor wanted to go out with him 'to do some shaking' that night. I admit that I had a more difficult time relating to Tor because I invariably associated him with Thor the Nordoom. If you are ever in the West Forties, you may run into Thor the Nordoom, as I did several times. If you do, you will have no trouble recognizing him. He is seven-feet-tall, wears a natty Viking costume, holds a spear in his hoof (*sic*), and carries mimeographed Visigothic poems in a take-one box hung around his neck. I think they were Visigothic. I never had the nerve to take one. Had I been able to communicate with Tor, I might have learned a good bit about my company. He must have had a pretty good idea what was going on because he borrowed small amounts of money from about a dozen of us in the office shortly before the going got rough and then disappeared, presumably back to Sweden. Never trust a sixty-three-year-old mailboy with a sociology Ph.D.

Young Randell, crew-cut and three-pieced, expressed his expert conception of the youth market for *Business Week:* 'We go for the clean-cuts on the other side of the barricades. Those other 5% are not our customers, and they won't be. We don't sell marijuana, LSD, or jeans...' JEANS? Even Agnew hasn't knocked jeans yet. And, of course, Cort later grabbed the opportunity to acquire a profitable company specializing in pants a lot freakier than jeans.

So it is perhaps a little generous to think of NSMC as having been in touch with the youth market, the expert in the field. But the original NSMC – the core company – was a profitable group of effective media NSMC had developed to reach this market. Or was it? The following italicized information was distributed by Farley Manning Associates, Inc., as public-relations background material for NSMC:

> [NSMC] *employs more than 700 paid student representatives.... Selected from top-calibre students,* [they] *have direct contact and therefore credibility with fellow students, which largely accounts for the great success of NSM programs. They are a vital factor not only in sales, but in research and sampling, enabling NSM to obtain up-to-the-minute, incisive data on the buying needs and moods of the student market.*

Does that give you the impression they get a weekly salary of $20 like the TWA reps? The reps were *not* on the payroll and were compensated only by commission or for occasional special projects. The plan: The NSMC rep would have so many exciting, lucrative projects that he would hire fellow students to assist him and become the manager of a thriving campus business. He would earn a few thousand dollars and pick up valuable business experience. Before graduation he would hand-pick and train a successor; after graduation he might come to work full time for NSMC.

In fact, 90% of the reps' activities involved handing out literature of one sort or another, which proved to be even less lucrative than educational. That some of the reps really were top-calibre students or credible with their fellows did not greatly enhance their effectiveness in handing out brochures. Most of their remaining time was spent complaining to NSMC about the continual logistical foul-ups that spoiled their chances to earn commissions or delayed their commission cheques when earned. After all, it isn't easy to keep track of 700 part-time employees who change addresses twice a year, who go on vacation and take exams at different times, who have little to lose if they are unreliable. Say Stan Wilson, the rep at Wofford College in South Carolina, decides to move off-campus for spring semester. He sends a postcard to his regional manager in *Knoxville* with the new address. Knoxville has to let the *New York* office know, because it is from there the reps are coordinated and sent instructions (things may be temporarily delayed as the office moves from the Time-Life Building to 345 Park Avenue). New York has to tell *Chicago,* because that's where the reps' handouts are printed, computer-coded, and mailed out; and *Washington,* because that's where the mail orders come back to be fed into the computer and credited to the reps' commission cheques. Somewhere along the line Stan's new zip code is accidentally mixed up with his computer code. This delays the delivery of the multi-savings envelopes he is supposed to hand out, and credits his commissions to Bob Hill, the conscientious rep at Babson Institute. Stan becomes disenchanted and takes a job in the cafeteria; but the computer keeps sending him tons of multi-savings envelopes, which he uses in his fireplace. Eventually, the computer flags the total lack of sales from all those computer-coded envelopes and alerts management, who promptly fire Bob Hill.

Luckily, investment analysts never bothered to poll a random sample of NSMC reps.

Problems with the campus rep system were not all logistical. College stores were generally hostile to our competition, which they tended to overrate. They saw our reps taking away their business and perhaps leading to the opening of competitive stores on every campus. When the college-store managers gathered in Las Vegas for their annual convention, the NSMC threat was the major topic of discussion (followed by shoplifting and the propriety of holding the convention in Vegas). An obvious form of possible retaliation for the stores would be to cut back on purchases from such NSMC subsidiaries as Colad, Campus Pac, Lewis Brothers Ceramics (beer mugs), Poster Prints, and others that depended heavily or entirely on these stores for their sales. Thus the campus rep system was not only a money loser in itself. It threatened subsidiary profits as well.

> *Carefully and skilfully structured, the NSM marketing system supersedes any traditional definition. Its programs can be easily altered daily to match the dynamics of the market it serves. More conventional approaches can be out of touch with the 'now' generation and may respond less quickly to produce the original and flexible programs required. Something new and now is needed to capture the interest and imagination of the most educated, affluent and critical generation the world has yet known.*

I am trying to find the p.r. man who wrote that eloquent passage. I want him to do my obituary when the time comes.

> *NSM has achieved outstanding marketing successes, both for itself and its clients, by combining new forms of media with existing ones in an integrated pattern, not yet attempted by any other organization serving the youth market* [for good reason?]. *Client utilization of these media provides NSM with a major source of revenue.*

Most clients were not willing to pay a fixed fee for NSM media services. Instead, they paid a percentage of the mail-order sales of their product. That way NSMC bore the full risk of the mailing or the handout or the poster, and the client had nothing to lose. Lots of people were willing to let NSMC handle their products on a percentage basis; it was much more difficult to find people to plunk down the $20,000 NSMC charged to post 20,000 posters. In the case of the American Airlines youth-fare card, for example, NSMC was allowed to keep most of the $3 sale price for each card sold. American was interested in getting its cards into the wallets of the youth market, not in profiting from the sale of the card. NSMC press releases that described American as NSMC's largest client ($700,000) did not mention that most of these revenues were derived from these $3 commissions, rather than from regular paid advertisements. Yet such releases were in part designed to persuade other companies to buy regular paid advertisements in NSMC media. NSMC wanted regular paying advertisements instead of mail-order deals, because it generally cost NSMC more to make a mail-order sale than the sale was worth. You can sell a lot of dollar bills for 90c.[1]

> *Many of these media forms are working tools used by students throughout the school year, offering advertisers frequent, long-term exposure at relatively low cost.*
> *Typical advertising vehicles include:*

I have learned that 'include' is p.r.-ese for 'here is everything we've got, and then some.'

> *Campus telephone directories (in constant use by students as well as faculty).*

---

[1] My high school bookstore manager used to say of the refrigerated Charleston Chew candy bars we used to crave, "We lose a penny on each one but sell so many we make a profit." He also used to say. 'Many are cold but few are frozen."

In my opinion this is indeed a fine advertising medium, though NSMC could offer it on only thirty of the nation's 2,000 campuses. I will describe NSMC's plans for nationwide expansion of this medium in the next chapter.

Freshman photo directories (an indispensable aid to campus social life).

One of my programs. No national ads had been sold in this medium, which reached forty colleges and universities at random, and something under 1% of the student population.

Wire-bound notebooks and other graphic materials sold through college stores (covers, inserts and tear-off coupons are utilized).

I don't know what was meant by the last fifteen words of that statement; but I do know about the wire-bound notebooks, which were my responsibility. I secured the cooperation of manufacturers of wire-bound notebooks to insert a page of advertising material we would supply for the front of their books. *Time* had pioneered this marketing idea, so it was bound to work for us. That *Time* was cutting back their use of this medium and that the margins we worked on were much smaller than theirs signalled 'caution'. But caution is not glamorous.

I went glammering around the country trying to set things up, which required some coordination. No notebook manufacturer wanted to be the first to join the program, and they all wanted to see the insert before making a commitment. At the same time, we were recruiting products and services to feature on the different versions of the insert and trying to obtain the necessary advertising copy. The final inserts had to be approved by the manufacturers, the advertisers, five or six NSMC executives including Cort, and the National Association of College Stores, in Oberlin, Ohio, who vetoed the record-club offer at the last minute for fear of competition with their stores' record sales. The art was being done by our short-lived art department, conveniently located in Oakland, California.

All activity had to be scheduled around the press time we had reserved at I.S. Berlin, our Chicago printers (and informal bank – at one time we owed them something like $500,000; but it was okay, perhaps because some of their people held a fair amount of $6 NSMC stock). Oakland, Oberlin, Chicago, and New York were all tied into a Telex system and we had a good time trying to send messages so cleverly abbreviated as to be indecipherable, on the pretext of saving money. The schedule got so tight I had to fly to Chicago to check the proofs, total elapsed time of my round-trip mission being six hours, thirteen minutes. It was on this outing that I learned Gutenberg's third law of printing: If you perforate a coupon on one side of a sheet of paper, you will invariably and irrevocably make an equal and opposite perforation on the other side. Man learns by his mistakes.

We printed 4.5 million four-colour inserts, which was frequently publicized, and, as usual, did not receive enough mail orders to cover our printing costs. There were no paying advertisers, only commission arrangements.

> *Book covers (carrying advertising distributed free to students).*

This was a program of local advertising on the outside of book covers designed for individual schools in California. The program lost money and was killed around the time this press release was written.

> *Calendar desk pads, highlighting campus events (also free; with attached advertising messages and send-in coupons).*

This medium was also the subject of a two-page spread in NSMC's second annual report, which didn't mention that the program was being terminated because it was unprofitable or that in order to accommodate a lot of advertising the desk pads were larger than most student desk tops. Instead, a 'case study' was described: 'A special 25c offer of [Schick] Krona-Chrome blades and razor was carried on 200,000 desk pads with perforated tear-off coupons in the form of self-mailer postcards. Result? Only a month after the distribution of the desk pads, there was a return of over 10%....' That is true, as far as I know, except that they forgot to mention (why complicate things?) that Schick actually ran several different offers on those desk pads, including one for *free* blades and razor. One might suspect the bulk of the response came from this terrific offer, which did not even require an envelope or postage stamp. One of my very first assignments for the company, by the way, was part of what they called the EEGADS program – Every Executive Goes And Does Something – for which I had to distribute a couple thousand desk pads uptown at Columbia. I may never forget the squadron of giant folded paper airplanes that flew out the dormitory windows in response to my efforts.

A summer-employment guide is also a popular medium for client communication at the end of the spring term.

I supervised this one, too, which happened to be the project that got Cort started in 1964. Read the italics again and then note that there was absolutely no advertising, paid or commission, in this listing of summer jobs – printed in December, not at the end of the spring term.[1]

My only accomplishment relative to the summer-employment guide was in helping to persuade the company to kill it, even though it was Cort's pet. Although it probably never was profitable, the project became ludicrous as half a dozen tiny competitors, assuming it had been the first step in NSMC's formula of success, copied it. With six companies flooding the campuses with ads for roughly identical guides – and a relatively constant number of potential

---

[1] In one of the early editions there had been an ad for an employment agency.

customers who didn't need more than one guide – NSMC's share of the market was cut by about two-thirds, while sales and production costs increased. Of course, the other problem was that with so many students buying guides that listed a relatively small number of jobs, mostly for camp counsellors, the students had little chance to be hired and the employers were deluged with applications. One camp we listed wrote that 400 applications had been received for three openings. Would we please not list him any more?

Posters with coupons attached, placed on school bulletin boards and in areas of heavy student activity, are seen nine times per week by the average student.

What Jeff Tarr may not have known about his Operation Match posters was that the commissions NSMC made from sales were nowhere near enough to pay their costs. Meanwhile, NSMC may not have known how difficult it was for Operation Match to meet its costs out of its share of the revenue. NSMC bought Operation Match and was thus able to suffer losses from both the selling end *and* the fulfilling end. When Al Hutton, our computer man, was given the pieces to pick up, he recommended the program be dropped.

The figure of 'nine exposures per average student per week' for this medium is credited to A. C. Nielsen, the TV-rating people. None of the NSMC marketing people I knew believed this figure, which they explained in various ways. The rumour I chose to believe was that special NSMC field men had been sent to the 'sample' campuses Nielsen had selected, to put up extra posters the day before Nielsen arrived. Whenever we complained about the continuing use of this questionable statistic, we were assured (I think sincerely) that it would stop. And yet it kept showing up all over.

When asked whether universities didn't mind commercial posters on their bulletin boards, Cort explained how in most cases the campus reps would go to the administration, describe the New York-based company they represented to earn their tuition, and obtain a rubber 'Approved' stamp to use on the

posters that semester. No doubt that was what Cort had en-
visioned when he set up the system. Perhaps it was suggested
to reps in their instruction manual. Cort may actually have
thought it was the truth. However, if more than twenty-five
of the 700 reps had such a rubber stamp, I would be one
surprised Foosball enfoosiast. In fact, many of the posters
were ripped down within hours of posting by janitors or competitive student reps.

The list of unprofitable and ineffective media continues in
much the same way. Nor was this optimistic style of writing
reserved for press releases. The first annual report described
among other novel media:

> Transplex – Mobile Marketing. This activity was set up
> during the year to offer a new medium to advertisers,
> manufacturers, and institutions.
>
> Transplex Mobile Units operate nationally, regionally, or
> locally. They are specially designed to stimulate interest
> in existing products, services, and ideas and to introduce
> new ones in new ways.

It's a little vague, and a picture would have helped, but when
I read this I saw a fleet of psychedelic trailer trucks rolling
from one campus to the next. I was reminded of HSA's Ollie
Orbit Mobile Ice Cream Truck venture.

How many mobile units do you think were out there making
money for NSMC? None, ever. A visionary leader of a
visionary company with a visionary public-relations firm may
state something not as it is but as he hopes or plans it will be.
Had he been challenged on such a statement after Transplex
plans were scotched, Randell might have replied: 'We fully
expected Transplex to be operating by the time the report was
published and were indeed prepared to service clients as
described. Unfortunately, we found that Transplex was not
what our clients needed and decided it was in our shareholders'
best interests to allocate our resources elsewhere. When you
are developing as many new approaches as we are in a market
as elusive as the student market, some are bound to fail.' To

remind the challenger just whom he was challenging, Cort might have added with a condescending smile – 'After all, we must be doing something right.'

The media NSMC developed internally were almost uniformly unprofitable (though the media NSMC acquired, Campus Pac and Mailbag, were well respected, established and profitable). But they were retained and highlighted so that Wall Street would understand the brilliant marketing system designed to exploit the huge youth market and dramatically increase the earnings of acquired companies like Colad. NSMC never worried about competitors like Class who were copying their success formula, because the formula so clearly led to red ink.

The challenge was to retain all these unprofitable programs and still report a profit to Wall Street. The challenge was met for quite a while by what is known as *creative accounting* and perhaps by what one high-ranking executive once termed 'near-fraud'. (This V.-P. earned the nickname 'Our Cheerleader' by overstating successes and understating problems.)

The first annual report NSMC issued in 1968, five months after the stock went public, showed sales of $5.5 million and pre-tax profits of $700,000. I was very proud of it and took it home to my room-mate Humphrey. He read the footnotes (how dull, I thought) and asked some rather nitpicking questions (obviously prompted by envy). In retrospect, his most important question may have been, 'What is this $1.8 million of 'unbilled receivables'? I've never heard of "unbilled receivables".' I hadn't either, and the footnotes didn't really clear it up. As best we could tell, this represented money clients had committed for programs that were nearing completion and would be billed soon. Anyway, Peat, Marwick, Mitchell's standard letter was on the last page saying they thought the report fairly represented our financial situation, and that was that, as far as I and my then $190,000 stock option were concerned.

I learned much later that $400,000 of the $1.8 million unbilled receivables Humphrey noticed were eventually received and that the rest would never be billed nor received.

The figures may have been off; but I believe that was the gist of the true situation. Clearly, the announced earnings of $700,000 in 1968 would have suffered somewhat if NSMC hadn't reported $1.4 million of sales that never materialized. As far as I know, NSMC never reported costs that didn't materialize, only sales.

But in stretching things a little, NSMC management may have been reasoning: 'We've promised Wall Street a dramatic increase in profits. If we don't show it, our stock collapses, we can't make acquisitions, we are stuck trying to make a profit internally (ha!). So we owe it to ourselves and our shareholders to be as liberal as our auditors will allow. And maybe even fudge a little. If it turns out that some of these hoped-for sales don't come through, the write-offs won't make a very big dent in *next* year's statement, because by then we'll have millions of dollars of acquired companies' earnings with which to absorb any of this year's rough edges. After all, our basic concept is sound and what big company didn't have to scramble a little when it was small?'

Speaking of unbilled receivables, I should recount an incident that seemed harmless enough at the time. We were still located in the Time-Life Building and all indicators were pointing up. Over the last few weeks we had heard progress reports of negotiations with Pontiac for what promised to be our first million-dollar contract. The deal seemed to be in that strange limbo stage where it was certain but not definite. (We had a lot of deals like that.) I was stretching my legs around ten o'clock in the evening and found that the only two people left in the office were Cort and a secretary. Cort was seated at a typewriter rattling off about three and a half words a minute. Always on the lookout for brownie points, and incensed by the idea of our leader wasting his valuable time, I let it be known that I was the fastest two-finger typist in the world. They were relieved to hear this, because the tricky spacing on the IBM Executive typewriter was giving them trouble.

Cort gave me a brief letter addressed to NSMC on Pontiac letterhead and explained the silly mix-up that had occurred.

You see, this was a letter confirming Pontiac's intent to spend something over a million dollars with us in the coming year. It had been received just in time to meet the accounting deadline for one of the financial statements (it wasn't clear how the accountants would use this document, just that it was important). A ridiculous typographical error had been made by the Pontiac executive's secretary. She had hit a *t* where she should have hit a *w*. Instead of a sentence reading, 'We are no*w* planning to spend umpty-ump dollars with your programs' (or words to that effect), we had a sentence reading, 'We are not planning to spend . . .'

Cort explained that the Pontiac executive had been reached by phone, had apologized for the error, had agreed to send a corrected letter, but upon hearing that the letter would come too late, had asked us to retype it for him. I cannot recall whether I asked or was told how the executive's signature was going to arrive at the bottom of the retyped letter. I do recall that I was supposed to match the format of the letter I was retyping exactly, with the exception of that silly typographical error. I did so, collected my brownie points and statements of wonderment at my dual digital agility, and went back to what I was doing. I imagine that the corrected text was pasted over the incorrect text on the Pontiac letterhead and that a Xerox was made and shown to the accountants – but this is no more than a guess based solely on the information I have related. Your guess is as good as mine. I have absolutely no evidence that the retyped letter wasn't entirely authorized by Pontiac. I also have absolutely no evidence that any of the Pontiac plans were included as unbilled receivables.

We wound up doing little or no business with Pontiac. They changed their plans.

In addition to the unbilled receivables, Humphrey was a little worried about the $486,000 shown as the 'unamortized cost of prepared sales programs'. A footnote explained:

> The company's business is seasonal and coincides with the school year. Expenditures are incurred for printing, lay-out, and mailing preparatory to the commencement

of various sales programs, most of which commence in the fall of the year and carry over into the spring.

The company follows the practice of deferring these costs and amortizing them over the periods in which applicable income is derived. The amortization periods commence with the various sales campaigns and costs are written off over the lives of the programs or a maximum of twelve months, whichever period is less.

In other words, this annual statement covered the fiscal year ending August 31, 1968. In August a lot of money was spent printing handouts and mailings that would not produce revenue until after August 31 – too late to be included in that year's income. So it was reasonable to defer the $486,000 of expenses to the 1969 fiscal year, since that was when the revenues from these expenses would come in. You can see, though, that reasonable or not, this would be a good way to postpone a loss if the $486,000 of expenses only produced, say, $150,000 of revenue. We will see more deferred costs in Chapter 9.

With my limited knowledge of accounting and the stock market, I was fascinated by one other interesting numbers game – the relationship of Cort's personal finances to his company's. For a while Cort owned 50% of the company stock, which was selling at 100 times after-tax earnings. His salary was $24,000. If he had raised it by $10,000 he would have had $10,000 more income, less perhaps $4,000 in taxes, or $6,000. But NSMC's pre-tax earnings would be $10,000 less, and after-tax earnings would be $5,000 less. Valued at 100 times earnings, this $5,000 reduction would mean a $500,000 decrease in the value of the entire company, of which Cort owned half. So, theoretically anyway, Cort's own equity in the company would decrease by $250,000. If instead he lowered his salary by $10,000, or $6,000 after tax, his stock would be worth $250,000 more. And when S.E.C. regulations allowed him to sell it, the Internal Revenue Service would consider that $250,000 a long-term capital gain, not ordinary income, leaving him $175,000 after taxes.

Thus, roughly and hypothetically, Cort might decrease his after-tax income by about $175,000 if he raised his after-tax salary by $6,000. And vice versa. Which may explain why Cort generously paid many travel and entertainment expenses out of his own pocket; paid low salaries and gave large options; and even gave away bits of his personal stock to avoid paying executives large salaries.

CHAPTER SEVEN

The Alchemy of Synergy

> Two and two may seem to make five
> when a conglomerate is making its
> pitch, but from what I've seen they are
> just playing a numbers game. . . .
> Don't expect lawyers or investment
> bankers to be objective about
> conglomerates. Visions of sugarplums
> dance through their heads at the
> mention of Gulf and Western.
> *Up the Organization*
> ROBERT TOWNSEND

The second image NSMC attempted to convey was that it acquired only outstanding youth-market companies whose earnings its marketing system could dramatically increase; that even without additional acquisitions NSMC earnings would grow at a phenomenal rate.

The word 'conglomerate' was ruthlessly suppressed at NSMC because conglomerates had by then fallen out of favour on Wall Street and were selling at even less than ten times earnings. (Gulf+Western had fallen from $50 to $12.) NSMC had to sell at about 100 times earnings to keep snowballing. The difference was that NSMC's companies all fit together in one market with obvious synergy – compared, for example, with the dubious advantages of linking Resource Publications to Paramount Pictures. And to some extent this was true. But the synergy thing was blown wildly out of proportion for Wall Street and prospective acquisitions. Both the practical and impractical opportunities were made to sound as though they either had been or were on the verge of being realized, which was far from true.

NSMC was only one of many conglomerates that did not consider themselves conglomerates. *Fortune* had this to say in an article entitled, 'Litton Down to Earth' and subtitled, 'It was great while it lasted. Then the legendary conglomerate collided with those everyday problems of management, markets, and costs.'

> ... [Litton executives'] reason for shunning the description 'conglomerate' (every conglomerate has at least one reason) is that the company, they say, has made its hundred or so acquisitions only in industries where its technological capability could give it a competitive edge. In truth, considerable mental agility is required to perceive an impending technological revolution in some of the businesses Litton has bought – e.g., office furniture. However, the company's plans for most of its divisions are convincing, and sometimes downright awe-inspiring.
>
> Litton is relentlessly future-oriented; its executives find it more congenial to talk about how their companies will be operating five years from now than about what happened yesterday. However, technological revolutions take time. Meanwhile, the corporation is saddled with a fair number of everyday problems.

Ironically, this article appeared the same month – April 1968 – that NSMC went public. If there was a lesson in it for potential NSMC investors, it wasn't learned, because exactly two years later – April 1970 – *Fortune* published an article entitled, 'How Cortes Randell Drained the Fountain of Youth' and subtitled, 'It looked great on paper – a giant conglomerate that would dominate the youth market. But when National Student Marketing's acquisition program ran out of steam, the founder was kicked out of his own company.' Wall Street being Wall Street, I expect *Fortune* will have no dearth of material for their April 1974, 1976, and 1978 issues, also.

At any rate, the idea was that NSMC acquired only outstanding youth-market companies. Speaking to the New York Society of Security Analysts about the kind of company eligible to join the NSMC family, Cort said, 'The company has to be the Rolls Royce of its category. . . .' It was characteristic of Cort to equate prestige and profits; however, this is a dangerous equation, as the bankruptcy of Rolls Royce sixteen months later attests. The Rolls Royce comparison is particularly unfortunate for youth-market companies, since the youth market does not spring for the highest-priced prestige item in a product line. But Cort wasn't really selling to the youth market (VWs and jeans); he was selling to the investment community (Rolls Royces and pinstripes).

As far as the 'quality' of the companies NSMC acquired is concerned, it could be argued that they ranged from poor to excellent. But were they really 'youth market'?

About half NSMC's business is in the youth market. Since half the nation's population is under twenty-five, this is not extraordinary specialization. The largest acquisition NSMC completed was Interstate National Corporation, which accounted for $1.8 million of the $3.8-million profit NSMC showed in its second annual report. Interstate is a diversified group of insurance companies based in Chicago with specialties in greenhouse, racetrack, and student insurance. You'll never guess which facet of Interstate's business NSMC stressed in its press releases; and yet most of Interstate's $20 million in revenues did not come from the youth market. While NSMC had plans to help develop the student end of the insurance business, complex state regulations and conservative testing procedures would have delayed any substantial programs at least two or three years. Interstate did show about triple the earnings in 1969 as it had in pre-NSMC 1968. But the increase was in no way caused by NSMC marketing talent. My guess is that it was caused in part by Interstate's desire to command a high price for their company and in part by NSMC's desperate need to show Wall Street the earnings it had promised; and that it was achieved in part by a liberalization of the accounting methods Interstate had been

93

using. It is doubtful that future earnings will increase fast enough to justify a glamorous multiple. Insurance companies are generally valued at about fifteen times their earnings, not 100 times.

Another $7 million or so of NSMC sales came from the Creighton Shirt Company, who did half their business in military shirts (a youth market of sorts) and the other half in a line of $10 to $15 dress shirts advertised in such student publications as *The New Yorker*. About $3 million more were from Mar-Clay Mills, Inc., a hosiery manufacturer that sold only to wholesalers. Knowing that Wall Street would be unhappy that Mar-Clay in no way specialized in youthful legs, NSMC decided to promote a student hosiery club that was 'expected to exceed 250,000' members. The club was a total flop, but it served its purpose, fitting Mar-Clay into the story at 100 times. Clothing companies are generally valued at about ten to fifteen times their earnings.

These three of NSMC's twenty subsidiaries were not the only ones that were nonyouth, with no practical opportunities for synergy I can think of, but they alone accounted for about $30 million of the $67 million in 1969 sales NSMC reported.

Perhaps to lower the age of the average NSMC customer and thereby conform more closely to the youth-market image, Cort acquired three school-bus companies and had plans to build a coast-to-coast system of these profitable companies. Thus a lot of kindergarten and elementary school students were added to our market. Always alert to synergistic opportunities, we thought of selling advertising space on the insides of our buses, much as the New York City buses do. We were discouraged by the large portion of our market that could not read, and by the limited discretionary income of such students. This was the kind of acquisition that might appeal to an investment analyst who didn't stop to consider it. Sure, school buses are right up their alley. No, we didn't know the first thing about school buses or six-year-olds or parents of six-year-olds or local governments and school boards. These companies were not selling anything to students; they were securing local government contracts.

NSMC's best known subsidiary was Arthur Frommer's little travel empire of *$5-a-Day* travel guides, $5-a-Day tours, and Arthur Frommer hotels. Once we acquired Frommer's company I stopped covering his books with copies of *Let's Go*. Instead, I decided to cover Fielding with Frommer and Fodor with *Let's Go*. This change in my bookstore-browsing strategy probably did more for Frommer's sales than most of NSMC's official attempts at synergy. When the *$5-a-day* books were offered on three million handouts (if only 2% generate sales, that's 60,000 books!), the results reaffirmed the old-fashioned marketing technique of selling books through bookstores. Although Frommer's company was exciting, and might have deserved a high multiple on its own, it was not youth-oriented. The books were popular with student and older travellers alike. Most of the revenue came from tours, which students generally avoid; and much of the growth potential for the company rested in Arthur Frommer hotels which, surprisingly, were priced well above the $5-a-Day budget Frommer symbolizes. I am told that when Frommer signed the closing papers, amidst popping champagne corks, trading ownership of his life's work for $6 million or so of unregistered NSMC stock, tears came to his eyes. No doubt they return whenever he thinks of that trade.

Five companies NSMC acquired afford a good example of the kind of synergy that was theoretically possible. All five were youth-market companies, though their combined sales equalled only about a fourth those of Interstate. If you had visited NSMC you might have heard something like this:

'An early acquisition was Shaffer Enterprises, Inc., in Kansas City, one of the two leading compilers of high-school-student mailing lists. Shortly thereafter we acquired National Scholastic List, Inc., in New York, which is the other. As competitors, each had to collect its own lists, feed them into the computer, and sell them. There was a lot of duplicated effort. Now we have split up the tasks and saved all that duplicated effort. This saving is all gravy – cutting costs without any reduction in revenue. Furthermore, as competitors these two companies were forever having to undercut each other's prices in the struggle for sales. Now we can hold the line. More gravy. [When I asked about anti-trust problems, I was told these companies were much too small to interest the Justice Department. I wonder whether a customer of one of these companies could sue successfully for treble damages.] In addition, NSMC's own sophisticated account executives, located in plush offices in New York, Los Angeles, the Prudential Center in Boston, the Hancock Building in Chicago, the Trade Center Building in Detroit, and the top floor of 1100 Connecticut Avenue in Washington, all represent these list companies when they present marketing plans to clients. Neither of the list companies alone could ever have afforded such an expensive sales effort; yet it costs NSMC nothing extra to include them in the sales presentations. Even more gravy! You see once a list has been compiled and fed into the computer it costs almost nothing to print out copies. So every additional sale of a list that would not otherwise have been made is nearly all profit.

'NSMC acquired Mailbag International, Inc., which sends young people millions of pieces of advertising material by direct mail for its clients. Of course, Mailbag is a big user of high-school-student lists and now obtains them internally at the substantial discount that prevails in intersubsidiary transactions. [The idea of increased profits from intersubsidiary discounts is a little misleading, since whatever saving one subsidiary realizes comes out of the revenues of the other. The only real economy may be not having to pay a salesman's commission on such sales. But this may be balanced by the diseconomies that often result when one subsidiary buys from another at a higher price (or lower quality or slower service) than would be available outside the family of companies out of a mistaken sense of loyalty – or even by order of the parent.] NSMC account executives also represent Mailbag. And NSMC products, such as the summer-employment guides, can be offered for sale in Mailbag.

'As with the high-school-list industry, there are two major companies that publish campus-telephone directories in this country. Again, we have taken the precaution of buying both. The directories are generally produced at no cost to the schools and are supported by local advertising. Listen to the list of synergistic opportunities these companies provide. First of all, the companies will save some of the effort and expense that used to be devoted to competition and will be able to share their expertise. Second, they both happen to be located in Lubbock, Texas, and will soon merge their operations with great savings in overhead. Third, NSMC has bound its colourful self-mailer envelopes, offering many of its own products, into these phonebooks at very low cost. Fourth, neither of these companies alone had a large enough circulation to be of much interest to national advertisers, nor the money or expertise to launch a national sales campaign on Madison Avenue. Consequently, they had to limit their activities to schools at which local advertising potential was great enough to support publication. Combined, these companies have a circulation of 850,000 books, which our account executives are now offering national clients. National sales will be almost pure profit on top of already profitable directories. And even more important, national sales will allow these companies to expand greatly the number of schools at which they can publish – since the combination of national and local ads will make many schools profitable that would have been unprofitable with local revenues alone. This in turn will expand circulation well beyond 850,000 which will become even more attractive to national advertisers.

'But that's not all. NSMC has purposely *not* acquired the companies that compile *college* mailing lists, even though Mailbag is a big user of these lists, too. Where do you think these companies get their lists? From campus phone directories! Shaffer will shortly be generating our own college lists at virtually no cost, since the same computer that sets type for our phonebooks will store these names and addresses for lists also. Our costs will be less than those of the existing companies, and we will have our lists ready several weeks earlier, since we will already be done by the time they get copies of our phonebooks!'

97

Wasn't that exciting? I think it was one of the best sets of synergistic opportunities NSMC had, especially when described that way. Some of that potential synergy was no doubt being realised. But these five acquisitions also illustrated some practical problems you might not have heard about if you had visited NSMC.

One major problem with acquisitions is that, like used cars, it is hard to know what you are buying until you have bought it. Especially if you are in a big hurry. Often a seller has good reasons for wanting to unload his company that are discovered only after the deal is done. Just as NSMC painted a rather rosy picture of itself to persuade companies to join the family, so some of the prospective subsidiary presidents may have been a little overoptimistic in their projections for the future, in order to command the best possible prices for their companies. Since the purchase price of a company is generally based on a multiple of earnings, there is the temptation to make this year look extra good at the expense of next year. One of the high-school-list companies turned out to be solid; the other had much more trouble meeting its projections.

If NSMC was unhappy about some of its subsidiaries, many of the subsidiaries were unhappy with NSMC. In practice, the NSMC account executives had little success selling high school lists or Mailbag mailings or national phonebook ads. Partly this may have been the result of the poor reputation NSMC had developed on Madison Avenue with its own media. Madison Avenue, to its credit, did not buy the NSMC story nearly as readily as Wall Street did. Perhaps Madison Avenue recognized some of its own techniques in the NSMC story.

This is a second major problem with acquisitions. NSMC was much better at acquiring companies than at keeping them happy once acquired. Unhappy subsidiaries can quickly sour – or at least put a damper on ambitious plans for synergy. This was particularly dangerous for NSMC, which acquired mainly nonmanufacturing companies whose chief assets were human, not tangible. There was only so much top-management time to be allocated between acquiring new companies and working with ones that had just been acquired. Newly acquired companies probably expected the same flattering attention from Cort and his generals as they had enjoyed before the papers were signed. Instead, they were largely ignored as Cort went on to marry other companies into the family. Where was the magic marketing system that would bring new life to, say, Institutional Directories, one of the telephone directory companies?

The self-mailers NSMC was binding into the Institutional Directories phonebooks gummed up their binding machine and caused Jim Tinsley, the President, and 'Spider' Harris, Vice-President, much grief. This is the kind of nitty-gritty practical detail that proved troublesome to the realization of NSMC visions. And as usual, the number of mail orders from these envelopes was nowhere near sufficient to cover the cost of printing the envelopes. (By the same token, printing up fliers to insert in Mailbag to advertise the summer-employment guides just increased the deficit in that charter NSMC program.) The idea of using NSMC's calendar-desk-pad ad salesmen to sell local ads for Institutional Directories at the same time never materialized because the Manager of that program was mainly interested in calendar-desk-pad profits, not in Institutional Directories profits. And it's hard to coordinate things from 1,500 miles away – another major obstacle to synergy. Eventually, the calendar desk pads were discontinued anyway. The idea of combining Institutional Directories and the other Lubbock phone directory company under one roof overlooked a subtle human-relations problem. Having been competitors for years, the two company presidents were not on the best of terms.

I happen to be among the fortunate who visited Institutional Directories in Lubbock, 'Hub of the Plains,' where I saw my first flying sagebrush. (With fringes like that, who needed vacations?) When I arrived at Institutional Directories' unimposing plant, Spider figured Jim was probably at 'the club,' and we drove over there. Lubbock was ostensibly a dry town, but everyone belonged to a club. This one was a motel lounge, and sure enough, we found our man. As best I could tell in the semidarkness, Jim was just over eight-feet-tall, though he was somewhat shorter when he sat down. I drank my vodka Collinses – what kind of sissified drink is that, they wondered – as slowly as I possibly could. I am cursed with a two-drink limit and have learned never to drink in the middle of the day unless I am prepared to turn in at around four p.m. I finished my third (trouble) as they finished their fifth bourbon and branch. The conversation consisted mainly of their complaints about all NSMC had promised and not done. They openly disliked and distrusted NSMC, though they were pleased the stock had tripled. Luckily, the jukebox and frequent interruptions of fellow club members and the cocktail waitress kept the discussion from becoming too heavy. I finally got to sleep that night around four p.m.

A third major problem with acquisitions, closely related to the second, is keeping management motivated after you have made them millionaires. A man may be happy without being motivated. Most of the companies NSMC bought had been built from nothing by the creativity and super-hard work of one or a few men, not easily replaced. What psychological changes occur when ownership changes? When you have been paid, say, thirty times the profits you made last year?[1] Certainly, improving your profits will help the team you have joined to raise the value of your stock – but how much effect can one little subsidiary have? Isn't it time to relax a little and enjoy what you've earned? To give your employees the long-delayed raises they deserve? To hire that long-needed assistant? Can the parent company complain that your earnings are not increasing when they are not following through with their magic marketing system?

Of course, the subsidiary presidents had employment contracts requiring them to manage their companies for several years. Some had 'earn-outs' that allowed them to get more stock in relation to whatever improvement in their profits they

---

[1] One subsidiary owner, who had insisted on a partial cash payment for his company, reportedly stuffed $1.3 million in cash into a shopping bag and returned to his native land.

could show (the sort of thing Dan Goldenson had from Gulf +Western). But even an earn-out generally lasts only three years. What then? Subsidiary presidents seemed to be hard workers by nature; proud of their companies regardless of ownership; anxious to fulfil their end of the bargain. However, such assets are fragile. Each subsidiary President reported to an NSMC Group Vice-President, whose main job it was to keep good relations while trying to squeeze the best possible earnings from the four or five subsidiaries under his wing. Some of the subsidiary presidents reported to G.V.-P.s twenty or thirty years their junior; all the subsidiary presidents watched the remarkable game of musical swivel chairs that went on in New York as they were transferred from one G.V.-P. to another. 'We know it is trying to reorganize so often, gentlemen, but it is one of the prices we must pay for such rapid growth. By the way, I understand the stock went up another two points this morning.'

A fourth major problem: NSMC acquired a lot of small companies that had been able to get along with small-company book-keeping systems and small-company tax brackets. In order to function as a piece of a large company, more sophisticated accounting procedures had to be instituted; monthly reports had to be prepared and sent to the home office; projections had to be prepared and marketing plans developed. This extra work required extra expense. It may also have rankled small-company presidents used to their own independent systems. And, by lumping all the small companies' earnings together, some of the tax advantages of being small were lost by NSMC.

A fifth problem is that acquisitions are expensive. Except in cases where there is some productive economic reason for a merger, acquisitions seem a wasteful misuse of the nation's legal and accounting resources. It cost NSMC more in legal and accounting fees to acquire Institutional Directories from Mr and Mrs Tinsley than Institutional Directories earned in a year. (It doesn't have to show up on the books that way, the legal and accounting fees may be 'capitalized' – spread – over about ten years.) One complicating factor in this case was the decision of the joint owners to get a divorce in the midst of the acquisition procedure.

But at least Institutional Directories really was acquired. Several months after the larger of the two phone-directory companies had been placed on the official organization chart (included as one item in the NSMC press kit), it quietly turned out that the acquisition had not been and would not be completed. So much for most of the national ad potential, the increased circulation potential, and the college list potential. If even the best-laid plans can go sour, it is not surprising that many of NSMC's ad-libbed plans soured, too.

Several months more went by before a tornado struck Lubbock, Texas. Institutional Directories was directly in its path. I had heard of owners burning down their ailing companies for the fire insurance, but NSMC always did things on a very grand scale. . . .

In sum, not all the plans for synergy you might have heard about had you visited NSMC were in fact realized among these five – rather four – rather three? – subsidiaries.

The last proposition in this corporate image needs to be examined also: Even without additional acquisitions NSMC earnings would grow at a phenomenal rate. This was the stickiest point of all, because financial analysts did not balk at asking, 'How much of the earnings growth you are projecting will come from acquisitions that have not already been made?' In other words, is this mainly a chain letter or mainly a solid synergistic growth situation?

It is now clear, if it was not when the question was posed, that growth in corporate overhead was far out-stripping any possible growth in internal earnings. NSMC could hope to meet its earnings projections only by massive new acquisitions. What is corporate overhead? It is the money spent to keep the pieces of the conglomerate together; and, more important to NSMC's case, the money spent to keep up the images that allowed the multiple that allowed the acquisitions that made up the house that Cort built.

Corporate overhead is $750,000 annual rent on Park Avenue headquarters ($15 per square foot, compared with the $1 per square foot we had been paying at Harvard Student Agencies). It is $400,000 spent to furnish those offices, vacated a year later. It is similarly plush, if smaller, offices in Boston, Washington, Chicago, Detroit, and Los Angeles, out of which NSMC's highly paid account executives tried unsuccessfully to sell NSMC's unprofitable media services. It is the cost (about $1 million) of maintaining a nationwide campus rep force at a deficit to provide these media services. It is retaining a public-relations firm to announce such things as retaining a corporate-identity team to develop a new logo (NSMC was not going to be outdone by Gulf+Western). It is an annual report that costs $150,000 to compile, design, produce, and distribute, or about $10 per shareholder. Would you have preferred the money as a dividend? It is frequent company-wide audits, costing perhaps $100,000 each. It is a similar fee to the management-consulting arm of Peat, Marwick, Mitchell for help in constructing an organization chart of profit centres with a computerized system of control that did not work out in practice, at least in my area of the company. How do you fit a refrigerator-leasing company onto a standard monthly report form designed for a mail-order company? It is the legal, accounting, and production expense of preparing a 278-page proxy statement, rumoured to be the Ling-Temco-Vought statement a few years before. Remember 'Jimmy Ling, the merger king'? It is sending out expensive corporate Christmas cards, monthly youth-market newsletters, and a company newspaper. It is phonecalls from Cort's plane. It is writing off the expenses incurred in exploring the Transplex Mobile Van idea – which sooner or later must be written off. It is my salary!

Because corporate overhead was growing faster than internal earnings, NSMC's earnings would actually *decline* if new acquisitions were not made. Yet on November 5, 1969, Cort volunteered in his speech to the New York Society of Security Analysts that earnings per share would be $4[1] for

---

[1] Remember, I am stating all figures as though there had been no two-for-one splits.

fiscal 1970 (nearly triple the $1.54 in 1969) – 78% from internal operations, 5% from acquisitions recently consummated, 7% from an extraordinary item, and only 10% from acquisitions presently under consideration.

The stock jumped twenty points at that good news, increasing Cort's net worth by $6.5 million, the paper value of my options by $80,000, and of Maggie's by $4,000.

Subsequent events indicate that Mr Randell was either fooling himself or fooling the public with that projection.

CHAPTER EIGHT

10,000 Refrigerators and a Side Order of Fries, Please

Dear Mr Simmons:
Any refrigerators you are able to lease
on our behalf will, I assure you, be
most artfully depreciated . . .

Okay, Mr Smart-Ass Vice-President, what were you doing all this time? Why didn't you blow the whistle?

One question at a time, please.

I was working seventy hours a week, trying with little success to justify in my mind my salary, now up to $22,500, and my stock options, now theoretically worth close to $400,000.True, my youth-fare card had expired and I was no longer a kid; but I felt such compensation was very generous all the same. Every weekly paycheque reminded me how beholden I was to Cort and the other members of the NSMC team, for which I tried to compensate by working like crazy; and how beholden I was to Eloy Velez and his two or three billion peers, for which I tried to compensate with guilt cheques

I felt beholden to Eloy because, given equal aptitudes, equal drive, and equal work, he could never hope to enjoy anywhere near the physical and psychological comforts that I did. This did not seem fair. Of course, I knew that the Declaration of Independence referred specifically to *Americans* when

it said 'all men are created equal,' and I was aware of the
international exchange rates as published (implicitly) in *The
New York Times* and the *Wall Street Journal* on a regular
basis (see pages 108 and 109 for recent quotations). I knew
it was more important to spend a dollar for milk in
Appalachia than a dollar for milk in Ecuador, even though
the dollar in Ecuador would provide ten times as much milk
(leverage?). The reason, I knew, was that one Appalachian
was selling at the rate of 1.6 to an American businessman –
or at a multiple thirty-seven times better than an Ecuadorian,
who was selling at 58.5 per. In other words, unless the dollar
could buy at least thirty-seven times as much milk in Ecuador
as in Appalachia, it would be better spent in Appalachia.
More important than spending that dollar for milk in either
place, I knew, was spending it for guns to maintain the
balance of power. After all, I knew the international human
monetary system rested on the stability of the American white
collar, whose value must be protected at all costs. If the
Ecuadorians want to live the way we do, why don't they stop
watching TV and playing golf and get to work?

I knew all this; sentimentality and that high school trip to
the Soviet Union got in the way of reason.

I asked $20,000-a-year Humphrey whether he thought the
system was fair. He said no, probably not. I asked him
whether he gave any of his money away. No. Didn't he feel
responsibility to those less fortunate than he? No, what had
they ever done for him? But people are starving to death!
Name one. I can't, but if someone were starving to death at
your feet, wouldn't you help him? Sure, but people don't
starve on the second floor of Upper East Side apartment
buildings – the doormen won't let them up. But if you would
help someone if he were starving here, why won't you help
him if he's starving in India? If I did, he would just have
five children who would be starving, also, and the problem
would get worse. Then why not support a birth-control
organization? I would prefer to spend my money on myself
and my friends. But they're wealthy, too. That's why they're
my friends.

Dammit, Humphrey, you keep joking about this as a defence because you feel guilty about not helping these starving people – be serious! What makes you so sure these people will be happy when they have enough to eat? Some of my richest friends are the unhappiest. Look, Humphrey, the physical agony of hunger is a lot worse than boredom or some psychological unhappiness. Well, $2 billion of tax money, mine included, goes to foreign aid. But that's only $10 from each American and $1 for each malnourished human being – and the military budget is fifty times as large. Hey, this is getting boring; let's go out for dinner. But what if everyone were like you? Then we wouldn't have any poor people – let's eat.

The remarkable thing about Humphrey was the warmth and generosity he showed his friends. He did think he would probably give some money away when he was really rich (how rich is that?), or in his will, and he pointed out that by investing his money wisely now, he could probably have more to give in the long run than if he gave a little each year. Humphrey was a little to the left of most of the budding millionaires at NSMC. And while I was considerably to the left of Humphrey, I was hardly denying myself toys in my crusade to save the world.

Part of my job was reviewing all the new products people wanted NSMC to market. I explained traitorously to most of them that what they had read about NSMC was misleading. We could not market their products. Our student reps did not sell things. We did not have a distribution network to retail stores. There were no Transplex vans. To soften the blow, and to indulge my chronic consumptionitis, I would often buy a few whatevers for the apartment. Unbeknown to my visitor, I would slip out of my mild-mannered Albert Schweitzer psychology into the decadent garb of Super-Consumer! Thus, the ten inflatable bottles, the inflatable toothpaste tube, the inflatable banana and the inflatable chair; the five Whisperlites that flashed on when you talked to them or when the psychedelic phone rang or when the colour TV was on; the two Infinity Cubes that are not easily defined; the

---

International Exchange Rates

Closing Averages+, + +   *July 3, 1971*

1 AMERICAN BUSINESSMAN=

		CHANGE			CHANGE
1.6	Appalachians	. . .	58.5	Ecuadorians	−.6
61.2	Armenians	+1.1	89.1	Estonians	+.2
6.8	Austrians	+.1	142.8	Ethiopians	+1.7
6.6	Belgians	−.1	4.9	Frenchmen	−.1
2.3	Britons	. . .	6.2	Germans (W.)	. . .
67.0	Bulgarians	−.3	139.4	Ghanaians	+2.0
2.3	Canadians (excl. Fr.). . .		112.4	Hondurans	. . .
98.6	Ceylonese	−.7	4.6	Indians (Amer.)	. . .
246.0	Chinese	+3.2	697.3	Indians (Ind.)	+9.2
*	Communist Chinese		5.0	Israelis	−.1
125.4	Congolese	+.4	7.3	Italians	. . .
85.7	Czechoslovaks	+.2	11.6	Japanese	+.2
27.5	Danes	+.1			

*These are not hard currencies available through normal market channels. Reports of recent black-market transactions set the exchange rate at about 14,600 to 1, though this is expected to fluctuate dramatically due to market illiquidity.

+Note: Exchange rates are compiled daily as a complicated computer-calculated function of the following factors: (a) distance of the people from Topeka, Kansas; (b) index of degree by which looks and language of the people differ from American; (c) index of degree to which the people agree with American policy/ideology; (d) overall supply of the people, (e) poverty of the people quantified in direct proportion to American guilt and resultant wish to ignore; (f) wealth of the people expressed as a function of potential market for American exports.

+ +Note: These closing averages are provided solely for the assistance of those concerned with hijacking, kidnapping, kill ratios and overkill quo-

---

International Exchange Rates (continued)

1 AMERICAN BUSINESSMAN =

		CHANGE			CHANGE
63.4	Peruvians	+.2	97.9	Jordanians	−.8
117.5	Polacks	−3.7	105.7	Kenyans	−2.6
82.0	Russians	−.1	91.2	Latvians	−.3
583.1	So. Africans (com.)	−3.4	99.6	Lebanese	+.5
28.2	So. Africans (pref.)	+.1	123.8	Liberians	+1.4
111.7	So. Vietnamese	+1.0	71.2	Mexicans	−.2
156.6	Sudanese	−1.3	138.5	Moroccans	+1.1
194.0	Thais	+2.6	211.0	Nepalese	−.6
230.8	Tibetans	+3.5	102.7	Nicaraguans	...
60.9	Venezuelans	...	*	No. Vietnamese	
161.5	Yemenese	+.9	31.2	Norwegians	...
148.3	Zambians	−1.1	468.0	Pakistanis	+5.2
148.3	Zanzibars	−.5			

tients, foreign-aid allocation, brain drains, the slave trade, migrant-worker wages, birth control, human rights, immigration quotas, international adoption, prisoners of war, genocide, and the like. This paper assumes no responsibility for the accuracy or morality of these quotations.

MARKET WRAP-UP: The American white collar held its own today in moderately active trading, as losers and gainers pretty well canceled themselves out. As usual, the most active nationalities were the Middle East and Southeast Asia groups. Indian Indians dropped to the third straight low in succession, losing value relative to all nationalities except Tibetans, who suffered a relatively greater setback in response to the rumor that *Lost Horizons* would be dropped from the movie schedule of the Late Show.

Kalliroscope, which allegedly depicted the entire history of the universe if you were imaginative; the Tensolator that would get me into great shape with no effort on my part; the personalized newspaper headlines; the posters; the bumper stickers; the eight-track cartridge tape player; the stick-on art nouveau insects; the Budweiser wallpaper; the phosphorescent rubber balls; the electric yo-yo's,[1] the computerized scale that lit up my weight; the lead-lined belt that would have kept my weight down if I had ever used it; the two Pop Art furry rugs; the artificial trees; the four Big Bang cannons (I even bought war toys!); the countless different kinds of greeting cards; and the pinball machine. I told Humphrey we'd better increase our theft insurance. He said no thief had such poor taste.

It pained Humphrey to see me spend money this way. My stepped-up issuance of guilt cheques nearly drove him to tears. Humphrey wanted me to *invest* my money.

Although I had lost a lot more on my glamour stocks than the $2,000 I had made on my sixty shares of NSMC, I more or less made up the difference by selling my Mustang when I moved into the City. (A parking space would have cost as much as my apartment in Princeton had, not to mention the increase in insurance. The one night the car *was* parked in a City garage, my tapedeck was stolen. The garage owner

---

[1] I never got my pair of electric yo-yo's home. The day I acquired them I locked myself in the office and put a noose around my forefinger to see what I could do. I half died when I heard a knock on the window behind me (we were way up in the pollutosphere on the 15th floor at 345 Park Avenue; maybe a pigeon had had too much to breathe). My cat's cradle ended in a series of knots as I turned around to see a window washer motioning to me to open the little air vent at the bottom of the window. Could he try it? Uh, sure. I had visions of this guy yo-yoing with a hundred-foot string. Could he keep it? I was a little taken aback but said okay. The next day a second window washer manoeuvered his plank to my already clean window and asked whether I was the one with the yo-yo's. Yeah, I'm the one, but I only have one left. He didn't believe that and wanted a yo-yo for his daughter's birthday. Aw, come on mister, you gonna keep the yo-yo for yourself and not let my little girl have it? That's what he said. What he was thinking was 'You've got to be kidding me, buddy, with your fancy suit and fancy salary – is this what you do all day?' What could I do?

wouldn't even refund the $3.50 overnight parking fee. I hate New York.)

I decided to play it really safe with about half my money and invest in Ford at $43 a share. My broker said no, I should invest in Chrysler if I wanted an auto stock. I said it would be a memorial to my Mustang and that the stock was selling at a lower multiple than Chrysler at $68 so it had a better chance to go up. He prevailed and I brought Chrysler. That, apparently, was what Ford and Chrysler had been waiting for. Ford moved briskly to $52 while Chrysler immediately headed for $25.

Finally my chance arrived. I bumped into Humphrey on the way to the shower (seven days a week I was either asleep, in the shower, at NSMC, or in transit) and he told me about Nationwide Nursing Centres. One of the top men at Humphrey's distinguished firm had somehow gotten a chance to buy unregistered stock in this company for $8 a share, even though it was selling to the public for $22. Humphrey said it was all quite legal, that they expected the stock to hit $40 in a merger with a steel company (steel is used in the manufacture of nursing-home beds – synergy), at which point the stock would be registered and we could sell out. The top man was buying a pile, Humphrey's boss was buying half as much, Humphrey himself was buying half as much as that – and to help me recover from Chrysler he would arrange to get me 500 shares of my very own. Humphrey had gone to Princeton *and* Harvard Business, his bosses were tops in their fields, the Pink Sheets did indeed show Nationwide at $22 bid, and I became one of its smaller shareholders. Again I felt guilty that the man on the street had to pay $22, if he had gotten the tip at all.

I gathered that nursing homes were The Thing because red-suspendered Steve Berg, my Program Manager, bought a call on Four Seasons Nursing Homes shortly thereafter. It was around $80, and as soon as it passed $93 he would begin to coin it. I could see this was no Omega Equities, which as it turned out had been suspended from trading by the S.E.C. before my Blue Cross salesman friend could sell out.

I tried not to think of how wealthy I was – rather, was about to be – and devoted my life to developing new businesses for NSMC. Some I turned down. We did not import English taxis and buses for sale to fraternities. We did not co-venture with a Texas oil man who wanted to set up a national mobile gas station company, with our campus reps driving his mobile gas trucks. We did not hire 10,000 girls to sell a new line of cosmetics made from the gel of the leaves of the *aloe vera* plant, *à la* 'Avon Calling.' We did not develop a slide display for college-store windows that would alternate artistic (sports, sex) slides with commercial slides. Nor did we get very far setting up a speed-reading program, selling parents of college freshmen coffeemakers, or developing a network of high-school-vending-machine companies to place our posters on their machines.

We did launch two profitable businesses, however. One was a company that published freshman picture books. I was often called on to describe this project to prospective acquisitions as we sat around the conference table putting our best feet forward. 'A lot of older schools, like Harvard and Yale, have for years published pictorial directories of their incoming freshmen to help them get to know each other (and perhaps help deans identify rioting students). We have undertaken to publish such books at the many schools that have previously had none. It's not the kind of project most students want to handle themselves, because except for some introductory pages of maps, phone numbers, academic calendars, and extracurricular-activity information, the books are rather mechanical and uncreative. We hired fourteen part-time representatives, including some of our best campus reps, and four full-time representatives to propose this project to schools across the country. Forty have signed five-year agreements giving us the go-ahead.

'In late spring the schools sent us the lists of their incoming freshmen, whom we invited to send in their pictures, biographical information, and the $4 participation fee. The solicitation letters were written and printed by us with the school's approval, and sent on their letterhead. We compiled the books over the summer and delivered them in the fall.

'Because we produced forty books we were able to negotiate a much lower printing price than an individual school could. Our processing costs were lower, also. Although there were some bugs to be ironed out, this project was profitable its first year. Next year we expect to do considerably more books.'

Sometimes I would also mention the synergy we hoped to realize from our telephone-directory subsidiary, Institutional Directories. We were able to use their very appropriate name for our project, and we were able to say that we had previously published many telephone directories for schools across the country. This was helpful. The more significant opportunity for synergy was not realized, however. That trip I took to Lubbock had been intended to persuade Institutional Directories to sell their schools on the freshman picture-book project, while we would try to sell the telephone-directory idea as we sold picture books. Then, at schools where we published both, we could combine our efforts for local ad sales. Unfortunately, Jim and Spider were too upset with NSMC to pitch our project to their schools. And when we sold some schools on the phonebook idea, they essentially said they weren't interested. In fact, after a while they threatened to sue us if we didn't stop using their name. I wonder whether one subsidiary of a conglomerate has ever sued another?

To hear Cort tell the same story was a little frightening, though we eventually prevailed upon him to tone it down somewhat. He would rattle off something like this: 'You see, it only costs about $2 to print the book, so we make $2 on each freshman [but what about all the selling and administrative costs?] and once we have 500,000 freshmen participate [an impossible goal] that'll be $1 million profit – you know there are nearly two million freshmen in this country. But that's just the start, because you have sales to upperclassmen who need the book to see all the freshman girls and make dates. These are even more profitable sales because you don't have to put the upperclassmen's pictures in the

113

book. [For some reason, upperclassmen are loath to shell out $4 for such books.] So you might shoot for another $1 million pre-tax. And then there are the local and national advertisements, which are still more gravy. Think how much better it is to advertise in a book that will be used for four years than in a daily newspaper, which is quickly discarded, or the yearbook, which a student receives only as he is *leaving* the market. [I agreed with Cort that there was advertising potential; we only differed on how much.] By the way, we are exploring the possibility of printing all these books either at Colad or Institutional Directories, so we can keep the printing profit as well. [But neither company is equipped to do the job.] Our mailing company helps us design and execute the mailings. [No.]'

Cort's motto which was printed on little self-standing signs by Colad and distributed company-wide as the 'NSMC Corporate Philosophy,' was: 'Make No Little Plans: They Have Not the Power to Stir Men's Souls.'[1]

Nor did we dream up this business ourselves, which was often implied. Two students had formed a partnership publishing seven such books in the Midwest. They approached Cort to sell him advertising space. No, thank you, but how about selling your company? They were hired for stock options to carry out the project. That led to one of the most difficult business situations I faced at NSMC: It had been their idea for NSMC to do the project, though freshman picture books had been published as small-business ventures for years at some schools. They brought NSMC their experience, though it proved to be of dubious value, and worked part-time to build the project. As it turned out, lack of time or talent prevented them from handling the project as my boss and I thought it should be handled (and as their replacement was able to handle it). But do you let them go? How? And what settle-

---

[1] In reading the draft of this chapter it occurred to me that this quote might not be original, though it was never attributed to anyone. *Bartlett's* attributes 'Make no little plans; they have no magic to stir men's blood' to Daniel Hudson Burnham, a turn-of-the-century architect, but notes that the quotation is in doubt.

ment do you make? And have you stolen their idea? Or even if you continue their small salaries until big options come due – what if the big options turn out to be worthless after all? That $2-million suit is still pending.

We decided to replace these two fellows and chose Steve Berg, who had signed up many of the forty schools. Despite the massive confusion at NSMC during the critical months of this program's second year, he managed to expand the program to fifty-four campuses with a profit of about $50,000.

That would have made a meaningful contribution when NSMC was showing $700,000 profit – but the scale of things had been multiplied dramatically. We needed a bigger business to make a dent.

To that end, we developed University Products Corporation to lease compact refrigerators in quantity to universities and student governments, who would in turn rent them to individual students for the academic year. The impetus for this business came from a former housing administrator in Seattle, Al Moe, who was willing to combine his experience in college housing with ours in selling schools on the photo-directory project. HSA had rented refrigerators at Harvard; Al had rented them at the University of Washington. Most important, Al was willing to do the legwork. Al's enthusiasm was more resilient than Silly Putty, which is what held him for three months until the first lease was signed.

Most of the competition was restricted to one-campus operations that would rent compact refrigerators directly to students for $7 a month, or $63 for the academic year. We thought this was the wrong way round, since the actual mechanics of delivery, pick-up, storage, and the like could be done more effectively by a student group than an outside company. Our plan was to be the wholesaler or franchiser in this business and to set up the student government as our retailer or franchisee. This way, students wound up paying about half as much for the service and the student government made a very healthy profit to use for other student services. In addition to the brochures and sales aids to convince the schools to lease our refrigerators, we developed a kit of

115

materials and instructions to help the student governments operate the program on a day-to-day basis.

I spent most of my time on this project and we called me President. I think I was the only NSMC Subsidiary President who was not a millionaire, since I didn't own University Products Corporation and couldn't sell it to anybody. But I still had a couple of years left in my timetable. The fun of building the business was more than enough compensation.

When Al Moe signed the University of Oklahoma, we hired a second representative, L. E. Simmons. L. E. was a senior at the University of Utah and had worked part-time as an NSMC student representative, calender-desk-pad salesman, and photo-directory salesman. He calculated his net after expenses from these programs to be zero, or nearly so; but, like me, preferred almost anything to studying. So for a few months he flew around the Southeast entertaining student-government presidents and explaining our new refrigerator program, flying back to Utah occasionally for exams. Then he was awarded a fellowship to spend spring term at the London School of Economics and became a regular on Pan Am's 747 trans-Atlantic route. Fascinated by the new direct-dialing system between London and New York, he would call me at home once a week. All of these expenses came out of his own checking account. Having at the outset of the program been given a choice between company-paid-expenses-and-low-commissions or no-expenses-and-high-commissions, L. E. took the gamble. And won $11,000 beyond his $20,000 of pleasurably plush expenses for five months of 'part-time' work.

When L. E. signed the University of Mississippi, we hired three more representatives. One of the three had been Director of Housing and Food Services at the University of Oklahoma for twenty years. Having arranged for the refrigerator program at his university, he could both see the nationwide potential of the program and speak convincingly of its success when he presented it to housing administrators at other universities.

With more and more students choosing to live off-campus,

housing administrators were having a harder and harder time filling their dormitories, which they must do to avoid a deficit. While most universities had forbidden refrigerators in dormitories, we were able to convince many that refrigerators would make dorm life significantly more appealing, thereby helping to keep the dormitory occupancy up.

At many of the schools we visited, refrigerators had been outlawed on the grounds that the dormitory electrical systems were inadequate to carry such a load. We located Norcold, Inc., in Sydney, Ohio, whose compact refrigerator runs on a patented motor that draws much lower amperage than other refrigerator motors. Even the weakest dormitory electrical systems would not be overtaxed by this machine. If the Norcold unit had a major disadvantage, it was the noise it made when running. The exact noise level depended on the currency at each socket and the motor in each machine. Some were noisier than others. I chanced to meet one of our customers, who said she had petitioned to be excused from an exam on the grounds that her refrigerator was so noisy she couldn't study. Well, all refrigerators make noise, as do most radiators and most neighbours, so I didn't pay much attention to the problem. Our own apartment was large enough for a full-size refrigerator, so I had no need for a Norcold. Now, however, living in a Harvard dorm, I am reaping my just desserts. How noisy is my Norcold? Noisy enough to activate my Whisperlite at the other end of the room; noisy enough to draw comments from telephone callers such as 'What's that noise in the background?' 'Oh. Just a minute while I unplug my refrigerator.'

We decided to feature Norcold, and wound up nearly doubling their sales of this line. We were by far their largest customer. Yet we were treated as though Norcold were doing us a big favour by supplying us. I saw the power of a monopoly. No one else produced a refrigerator with such minimal electrical requirements, and this was the machine we needed. I began to see a pattern in the behaviour of New York landlords and Sydney industrialists. I had always thought selling was much harder than buying: I learned from Norcold that buying was no cinch either. Have you ever been to Sydney, Ohio, by the way? I went three times (no one from Sydney ever paid us a visit). My third trip was perhaps one of the highlights of Sydney's late-night life, as I drove my Avis Blandmobile over a cliff. Well, sort of a cliff. This was my third rent-a-car of the day. I had begun in Topeka at the photo-directory printer, flown to Norman, Oklahoma, to visit the University, and then (via jet through Ponca City? Stillwater? Enid? and Dallas) to Sydney, near Dayton. It was past midnight when I finally sighted my motel, which was the kind that had an adjoining gas station with which it it shared a black macadam parking area. Or so I thought until my car was balanced like a see-saw over the black macadam ledge that separated the gas station parking area from the motel parking area three or four feet below. No wheels touching the ground. The five or six teenagers who instantly materialized consoled me with the news that I was the third such imbecile of the month, and I got the impression that kids in Sydney looking for something to do after eleven at night would go to this gas station to watch cars go over the ledge. I gave the towers an extra $5 to paint the ledge yellow, but am in no hurry to return to Sydney to find out whether they did.

I can't blame the Norcold people for not liking us very much, even though we were buying their refrigerators. They were solid, conservative, Midwestern manufacturers with about thirty years seniority who, I think, were somewhat envious and sceptical of the NSMC instant success they read about everywhere. How come they, who were producing something tangible, were growing slowly, earning modest incomes, and facing all kinds of practical problems, while we young city-slickers, who produced nothing, were making our fortunes in three to five years?

In order to decrease our dependency on a single supplier, I decided to invent my own low-amperage refrigerator. The common characteristic of the GE engineers and others who had tried and failed, I knew, was their scientific background. It seemed logical to me that, not having that common characteristic myself, I would succeed.

Working from the knowledge that a magnifying lens placed between sunlight and a spot on the ground would singe the grass, I postulated that the lens was transferring heat from the area above its surface to the area beneath. I realized that the area above the lens was thus being cooled by the lens. I constructed a large glass box with a paper-thin top and a lens-thick bottom. This box sat on top of a black box. Sunlight passed through the thin glass top of the box reaching the lens bottom. The lens heated the black box underneath (an oven) and cooled the air directly above, which was entrapped by the top box (a refrigerator). The problem of cloudy days and dark rooms was easily solved by attaching a sun lamp that would hang over my contraption. Now it only remains to invent a low-amperage sun lamp. I will keep you posted.

In the first ten months of this program we signed long-term leases with thirty schools to whom we delivered about 10,000 refrigerators. Our little team of five representatives, Maggie (by now 'Administrative Assistant' rather than 'secretary'), and me saw a limitless future in refrigerators. We had already leased enough to stretch, if they were placed side by side in single file, from my apartment at 88th Street down to 345 Park Avenue, over to the old offices at the Time-Life Building, and down to Humphrey's office on Wall Street. We had a terrific reputation on campus as we helped students peacefully to overturn restrictions on refrigerators. Refrigerators meant breakfast in bed, drinks with ice, inexpensive and convenient snacks, better parties and bull sessions, and a little individuality in life-style. Well worth 7c per student a day, everyone agreed. Glowing front-page stories from the campus newspapers of our first schools helped to sell future schools. We had every reason to expect there would be enough University Products refrigerators on lease within three years to generate an annual pre-tax profit in the half-million-dollar ballpark and to stretch single file from my boss's $300,000 town house in midtown out to his home in Scarsdale and back.

But NSMC ran out of the cash needed to purchase the refrigerators, as I will explain later on.

And I remember now that I still haven't answered your other question: Why didn't I blow the whistle, call the cops, and have everybody hauled away?

CHAPTER NINE

The $3,754,103 Footnote

In our opinion, based upon our
examination and the aforementioned
reports of other independent public
accountants, the accompanying
consolidated balance sheet and
statements of earnings, retained
earnings and additional paid-in
capital present fairly the consolidated
financial position of National Student
Marketing Corporation and
subsidiaries at August 31, 1969, and
the results of their operations for the
year then ended, in conformity with
generally accepted accounting
principles applied on a basis consistent
with that of the preceding year in all
material respects.
Peat, Marwick, Mitchell & Co.

I naturally developed a number of different subrationaliza-
tions to my Great Rationalization that accounted for my playing along with NSMC, for remaining in the overheated
steamroom. Perhaps they are most easily described with
reference to a particular situation – such as the second annual
report.

August 31 was the last day of NSMC's 1969 fiscal year.
The second annual report could easily have been mistaken for

a copy of *Venture* magazine. Inside the embossed cover were sixty-four pages of mostly full-colour photographs describing a $67-million company going on $1 billion. The report was not saddlestitched with staples, like a magazine or pamphlet; rather, it was perfect bound, like a book. It was every bit as slick as reports of companies ten or even 100 times NSMC's size, and really put NSMC's best foot forward. But isn't a company free to spend what it wants on its annual report, to highlight good news and bury bad news in footnotes, to radiate optimism and confidence in the midst of difficulties?

The content of the report was much like the press release quoted earlier. For example, the $20 million of mainly non-youth-market insurance sales were described this way: 'The newest division, Financial Services, at this time provides health, accident, and affiliated insurance coverage to students, young travellers and campers.' The truth. Was the company required to describe the greenhouse and race-track specialties as well? The whole truth? I don't know. As usual, there was much that is misleading; hopes stated as plans, unprofitable projects about to be dropped described as ongoing, presumably successful. Nothing but the truth?

It didn't seem my place to tell our professional public-relations people just how far they could ethically go in applying make-up to the corporate physiognomy. Anyway, sophisticated investors usually consider financial statements the most important part of an annual report and disregard the trimmings just as naturally as a smart housewife notes the bones when she buys meat by the pound.

When NSMC's 1969 fiscal year ended (August 31), it was clear that the earnings projections Cort had made would again be impossible to meet without a little 'creative accounting.' He needed to show about $3.5 million in net earnings. Two problems were CompuJob, which you will recall lost a lot of money despite the good publicity it produced for NSMC, and the Canadian arm of NSMC. So on November 30,[1] 90 days

---

[1] This is the date I noted next to the footnote in my copy of the annual report, I can't remember whether this was the exact date, or an approximation. If an approximation, it was fairly close.

after the fiscal year had ended, an agreement was made to sell CompuJob back to Tan and Ed, and the Canadian operation to its managers. According to the footnote, 'In the opinion of counsel in both transactions negotiations and agreements of sale were in effect consummated prior to August 31, 1969 . . .' These transactions allowed NSMC to add $369,000 in after-tax earnings, or about 10%, to its 1969 results. The $369,000 represented the 'aggregate gain . . . as a result of the sale of the subsidiaries.' Where did Tan and Ed and the Canadians come up with the cash to buy back these subsidiaries? No cash. The footnote explains that payment was made with one-year and five-year personal notes. Even though NSMC didn't get any money in fiscal 1969, it was able to show in earnings the money that would come in over five years. Don't worry about the loans, by the way. The footnote says they are secured by 3,850 (original) shares of NSMC stock then valued at about $400,000, now valued at about $40,000.

How could something I saw everybody sweating over the night of November 29th have in effect been consummated prior to August 31? But I am not a lawyer or an accountant, and our lawyers and accountants were evidently on record saying this was okay. Moreover, the footnote was apparently sufficient notice to the public of what had happened.

I never learned what inducements persuaded Tan and Ed to take CompuJob off NSMC's hands. Whatever they were, the sale was made with so little fanfare that, while notice was being given in the footnotes of the report, CompuJob was mentioned in the big type up front as though nothing had happened. I whistled, all right, but at the system, not for the cops. I was beginning to see why a business-school (or law-school?) education might be helpful, after all.

Meanwhile, another footnote explains a new item on the balance sheet called 'deferred new product development and start-up costs.' Here was $533,000 that was spent in fiscal 1969 but that would be charged against the future, on the theory that at least $533,000 of revenue was likely to be derived in the future from those invested expenditures. Had such a sum been charged against 1969, earnings per share would have decreased by 10c per share (unadjusted for splits), and the stock might have sold for $10 per share less (100 times 10c per share), which would have made it more difficult for NSMC to acquire other companies. The same kind of calculation could be run for similar footnotes to show the relationship between an accounting decision and stock price. I am not saying NSMC should not have deferred this $533,000. That is a matter of judgment. Take my salary, for example, which may be included in the $533,000. A conservative management would probably have considered my salary an administrative expense and charged it against the period in which it was paid out. A go-go management would probably have considered my salary a research-and-development expense and tried to persuade the auditors to allow them to spread it out over the next three to five years. In the long-run, my salary would be charged against earnings either way. But to a glamour company, earnings now are worth far more than future earnings. I don't know how my salary was treated; but I think it illustrates some of the latitude a creative accountant enjoys.

The 'unbilled receivables' are back, up to $2,800,000 from the $1,763,000 shown in 1968 – only there is a twist. In the '1968' column of the 1969 annual report, which is shown for purposes of comparison, you would expect to see $1,763,000, as was reported in 1968. Instead, you see $945,000. This discrepancy is not explained in a footnote. Perhaps the missing $818,000 of 1968 assets had to be written off when it turned out they would not materialize.

You may recall also the $486,000 of 'unamortized cost of prepared sales programs,' which had been deferred in 1968 because these were expenses for printing up fliers and the like that would not produce revenue until 1969. Now that figure is up to $1,048,000. In other words, 1969 was charged with $486,000 that was actually spent in 1968; but 1969 was *not* charged with $1,048,000 that was actually spent in 1969. There are two ways of looking at these deferrals. If the $486,000 eventually brought in revenues of more than

$486,000, and if the $1,048,000 eventually brought in more than $1,048,000 – then this is an accounting method of 'waiting for profits.' Not counting your chickens, and all that. On the other hand, if the $486,000 eventually brought in less than $486,000 and the $1,048,000 less than $1,048,000 – then this is an accounting method of 'postponing losses.' Borrowing from the future with no hope of repayment, and all that. Of course, it is hard to predict future revenues, so it is hard to accuse anyone of purposely trying to postpone losses (which violates the Generally Accepted Accounting Principles). You can only accuse him of being groundlessly optimistic. It is the man who feigns optimism in order to postpone losses he expects who is cheating the system. While we can't tell for sure whether NSMC's optimism was feigned or genuine, it appears to have been unjustified.

And now we come to what I would like to call the Killer Footnote. This note points out that if you don't include in fiscal 1969 figures the earnings of companies whose acquisitions were 'negotiated and agreed to in principle before August 31, 1969, but closed subsequent thereto . . .' or the earnings of companies whose acquisitions were 'agreed to in principle and closed subsequent to August 31, 1969 . . .' – then you have to exclude $3,754,103 in net earnings, leaving a profit of $110,977, or about 4c a share (unadjusted). Dig beal, as they say. In other words, if you don't count companies that were not legally part of NSMC in fiscal 1969, then fiscal 1969 barely broke even. (*If* you accept the rest of the creative accounting.)

So why was the stock selling at $140 a share? The company earnings were valued at a multiple about ten times that of other conglomerates, and those earnings were apparently far from solid. A good time to sell, even though prestigious brokerage houses were still issuing 'buy' recommendations.

Brave Alan Abelson dared to point this out in his column in *Barron's*, and the stock fell twenty points the next day. Not so much because of what Abelson pointed out, but because people knew that when Abelson roasted a company, its stock fell about 15%, so they figured they had better sell

NSMC until it had fallen about 15%. This is an over-simplification, I admit; but widely read Wall Street columnists surely start as many trends as they discover. Their prophecies are self-fulfilling, too. It was rumoured, incidentally, that the NSMC annual report was brought to Abelson's attention by someone who had shorted[1] 3,000 shares of NSMC stock. If so, that someone made $60,000 the next day, and considerably more thereafter. Abelson had called the cops and the snowball began to melt.

NSMC's reply to the charge that earnings came from companies acquired after the close of the fiscal year was that considerable expenses were incurred in expanding the core company's capabilities in preparation for the acquisition of these companies. If their earnings hadn't been added, neither would the extra capabilities have been necessary. (I thought that might be a euphemistic way of describing the massive costs of running unprofitable programs in plush surroundings in order to have the kind of story that would command a 100-times multiple.) Moreover, the Chairman of Peat, Marwick, Mitchell's Ethics Committee was present at the NSMC annual meeting to read the portions of the accounting principles code that required acquisitions made shortly after the close of a fiscal year to be included in that year's statements.

People had begun to doubt, but Cort kept promising another tripling of earnings and, as you recall from his speech to the New York Society of Security Analysts, predicted that 78% of the higher 1970 earnings would come from internal operations, and only 10% from acquisitions that had not yet been made.

In any case, my first subrationalization for not publishing some kind of dissenting annual report was my not being sure, especially at the time, whether NSMC was exceeding acceptable limits of public relations, creative accounting, and

---

[1] Shorting a stock is the opposite of buying it. You sell it first, by 'borrowing" it from your broker, and buy it later at a lower price, if you are lucky, to 'pay your broker back.' While shorts are supposed to be restricted to stocks listed on the exchanges, in practice stocks traded over-the-counter are sometimes shorted also.

corporate law, though I imagined those limits were being severely strained at the very least. Although I assumed the accountants and lawyers were given unfalsified records to work with, I really had no way of knowing. All that was handled at the very top where hands are presumably always spotless. I also assumed that major accounting and law firms would not risk bending their standards for the sake of a client, albeit lucrative. While it was obvious that the public image was a rather fanciful description of the company, I presumed that dollars were dollars and documents, documents when it came down to the assets and liabilities of a financial statement.

A second reason for remaining loyal was that it seemed more reasonable and practical for a company to correct an unfortunate situation rather than commit suicide. Should GM encourage class-action suits against its failure to work sincerely toward curbing pollution, or should it simply begin working toward that end? We all complained frequently to Cort's inner circle about the way the story was being told. The inner circle in turn complained to Cort. We kept getting signs that things would improve, such as the appointment of a Chief Operating Officer, Roger Walther, who was a straight talker and who was willing to stand up to Cort. The third annual report would be different.

A third reason was that if I turned out to be *wrong* in my youthful idealism and/or NSMC and its mutual-admiration society withstood my attack, I would have had a rather difficult time being hired anywhere else. Patrick Henry for President, and all that. Fourth, I had already decided how to split most of my imminent fortune over various Eloy Velez-type projects. I was almost ready to believe that my then $400,000 stock options, with eighteen months down and six to go, would indeed be worth something. It might be stretching things to say I was beginning to see Ecuadorian towns renamed in my honour – but you get the idea. I wouldn't have minded the 20% I was going to keep for myself, either. My ego was raving over its new clothes – Vice-President of the darling of Wall Street. I, too, wanted to believe.

Fifth, I figured that even if Peat, Marwick and White and

Case were being fooled, there were a lot of insiders with more information and more experience than I to whom I could pass the buck. We had lured from Time, Inc., a seasoned executive who was billed as being in line for the Publisher's job; we had lured from J. Walter Thompson a Vic-President with a tremendous track record; we had in-house attorneys and financial people; we had computer people from IBM; we had two Harvard MBA's assisting Cort full time. Did I have the nerve to call a press conference and expose the American Business Establishment? Not *this* kid. I would wait and cast the *second* stone. And I do believe I would have been attacking much more than NSMC with such a press conference. I would have been attacking all those wild glamour stocks of recent years, all those highly paid shingle-hanging professionals, and all those aggressive young entrepreneurs who expected to make a fortune in three to five years, while 60% of the people on earth struggled to get enough to eat. I would surely have been branded as one of the radical left who wear blue jeans.

Finally, I was very proud of and involved with my own projects, which I felt were exciting. In presenting the NSMC story, as I often did, I was enthusiastic about NSMC's legitimate good points – there were and are many – but I don't think I knowingly passed on much of the fiction. Of course, by remaining an employee I tacitly endorsed the company. And I obviously did not stress the seamy side of the story as I have here. In the case of the one tiny acquisition it was my responsibility to complete, I spent hours with the company's President (Yale '68) to expose all the myths – self-fulfilling prophecies, ineffective media, the works. Yale or no, I wanted to be sure he knew everything I knew before betting his little company.

But it turned out there was a lot I, and virtually everyone else with the possible exception of Cort and a few top generals, did not know. Just when serious, secret negotiations were going on to acquire three huge companies – National Tape with $60 million in sales, Champion Products with $50 million, and Josten's, listed on the New York Stock Exchange with $70 million – acquisitions that would have assured NSMC's earnings projections and kept the ball rolling, the accountants finally found that something was very wrong and the lawyers advised NSMC to announce preliminary information to the public. On February 24, 1970, it was announced that there had been a loss of $1.2 million on sales of $18 million for the first quarter of fiscal 1970 – September 1 through November 30, 1969 – the year for which Randell had been promising tripled profits. Whatever confidence or credibility may have remained was obliterated two days later when it was announced that the company had made a 'mechanical error in transferring figures from one set of books to another,' such that the loss would actually be $1.5 million on sales of $14 million. Where was the sophisticated, computerized management-control system now?

Evidently, the net profit for all the subsidiaries in this quarter had been a respectable, if not synergistic, $2.2 million; but corporate overhead, the campus rep program and others whose losses could be deferred no further, and write-offs of some of the previous year's creative accounting had racked up a deficit of nearly $4 million.

I was in Cambridge on a rare three-day weekend when I first heard the news from my Yale '68 Subsidiary President. It came as a complete surprise. I had assumed from Cort's profit projections that subsidiary earnings would continue to be large enough to absorb the costs of keeping up the corporate image. Then I saw the silver lining: No doubt this was the great house-cleaning! NSMC was paying its debts to the future, getting its accounting back in line, starting afresh with a clean slate. I figured the stock would suffer for a while, but that a profitable second quarter might restore confidence. In any case, it was pretty clear that 1969 earnings had been boosted to Cort's projections only by dumping problems on 1970. Soviet factory managers do the same thing, borrowing a couple of days' production from April to meet March quotas, then borrowing three or four from May to hit April, and then a week from June to hit May. Since the managers purportedly meet their quotas, they cannot ask for lowered ones. If anything, quotas are raised. When the reckoning comes, as it almost always does, the Manager is sent off to you-know-where.

If 1969 earnings had not been thus boosted, the stock would have fallen that much sooner, before acquisitions like Cliftex could have been made. Cliftex is a sports-jacket manufacturer in New Bedford, Massachusetts, that NSMC managed to buy for about seventeen times its $1.2 million earnings, with 100-times-dubious-earnings stock. This one, and a couple of others, brought NSMC sales close to the $100-million level.

If 1968 earnings had not been thus boosted, perhaps NSMC would now have sales of about $8 – not $80 – million.

If 1967 earnings had not been similarly increased, NSMC might never have gone public in the first place. (In fact, on the suspicion that Cort's *own* business ventures never made a dollar of profit from the day he started, it was suggested we call this book *How To Succeed in Business Without Really Having One*.)

So the slate had finally been cleared, to the considerable embarrassment of the company. But had it? There was the possibility that this huge deficit was the minimum that creative accounting would allow, that the debt to the future had actually been increased to keep the deficit from being even larger.

The announcement explained at last why NSMC stock had been slipping so badly – from a high of $143 in December 1969 before the *Barron's* article appeared, to $72 the day before the February 24th announcement. The following day the stock dropped only another dollar.

The *Wall Street Journal*, which by now was running articles almost daily about the Street's favourite stock of 1968, asked Jimmy Joy, our appropriately named Financial Vice-President, just when company officers had first known there would be a loss shown in the first quarter. 'About January 20th.' And had anyone leaked the news to the investment community? 'Absolutely not.' Joy attributed the market's foresight to widespread speculation and rumour that things were awry.

Nothing affects the price of a stock more than its earnings. The first one to know about the loss NSMC would announce held valuable information. Because the first one to sell a stock trading at $143 a share probably will get about $143. But as more and more people start selling, the market price goes down. By the time the loss was announced to the public, you could only get $72 for your shares. The first kids in the lunch line pick out the best apples. The Securities and Exchange Commission is the lunch-line monitor. They get most upset when company 'insiders' act on information before it has been publicly announced. Someone will always be first to buy or sell his stock; but the S.E.C. wants to be sure that Irving Investor has some chance of a good place in line. Otherwise the officers of a company could buy their own stock, announce some good news so it would go up, and sell the stock before they announce bad news. The NSMC officers were probably not guilty of such manipulation when they sold more than $1-million worth of their personal stock as it passed its peak of $143 – but it's hard to decide what is insider-trading and what is not. (Insiders are supposed to file monthly reports with the S.E.C. noting any transactions they may have made in their stock.)

If a company officer gets the feeling that long-term prospects are not too good, and so wishes to sell his stock, must he call a press conference to announce his private doubts about the company's future? He might not get much of a Christmas bonus if he did. Must he hold the stock indefinitely and only sell when it has hit rock bottom? If the answer to both questions is 'no,' then what is the answer to this one: If he is right and the company begins to announce bad news from time to time, will he look bad having sold out before the fall? Yes.

So it's a sticky area for the S.E.C. to regulate, and a difficult one for insiders to deal with. This insider knew of the Interstate acquisition an hour before it was announced and (wrongly) could not resist the temptation of running down to a phonebooth and calling a good friend to recommend purchase of 100 shares. What better gift to a friend than an inside tip likely to be worth a few thousand dollars? What a great way to feel like a Big Shot. What a shame to let such a valuable opportunity go to waste! Who would find out about a measly 100 shares? You just found out. (As it happened, the market had already pretty much 'discounted' this news, and had pushed up the stock price in anticipation. It didn't do my friend any good at all. I guess I wasn't first in line, after all.)

At $72, I was only worth $100,000, but I would have gladly taken that paltry sum and retired to the business school or Bermuda if I could have. The Harvard Alumni Bulletin, to whom I had sent proud news of my Vice-Presidency about eight months earlier, managed to record it in the March number. Randell was having problems of his own. His net worth was down from $48 million to $24 million, but he must have figured the jig was far from up. Even after he knew of the loss, he continued to predict big profits for 1970. He did not know that the people had renounced their faith.

In fact, the day before he was forced to resign, Cort talked optimistically with one of my colleagues and recommended purchase of the stock. If you play hearts, you know it takes *all* the hearts and the queen of spades to 'shoot the moon' and score twenty-six positive points. Otherwise, the more hearts you have the more negative points you suffer. Once you let even a single heart slip, you've lost the moon and should pick up no more hearts. Yet how often have I, having developed the perfect strategy to the moon, let one heart slip but continued to collect the hearts, refusing to relinquish the fantasy and return to earth?

On February 10, Randell was reportedly asked whether he was worried that subsidiary presidents and his own key executives now held a majority of the stock and could force him out. He was quoted in *Fortune* as replying: 'Who do they respect? Their confidence in me to succeed is what brought them here. Why do people like Morgan Guaranty buy the stock? Because they have talked to Cort Randell and they have confidence in what we are trying to accomplish.

As long as I do a good job, I'll continue. If I don't do a job, I don't deserve to be President.'

How about this earlier passage from *American Way* magazine:

> We have a late dinner one night in New York at a midtown restaurant. Randell eats very lightly, as usual. He is introspective. 'I'm lucky,' he says, 'but there has to be some reason in life for this whole thing happening other than making money'. He comes close to feeling, he says, that providence has some different work for him to undertake someday. 'I feel certain I'll know what great project I'm to begin,' he says. 'I don't know what it is, but I'm sure that someday – within a year, or five years, or even twenty years, I'll be told.' As he talks this way it is not difficult to imagine him the founder of a philanthropic foundation, or sponsor of medical research, or college benefactor.

Can you blame a man who is told several times a day he is a marketing genius, a visionary able to turn his vision into reality, and an awfully nice guy – for believing some of it? There is no question that Cort was a self-promoter. Perhaps he was more eager to think great things about himself than most of us. The fact that Cort was 'deeply religious' (a church deacon) was probably also mixed into the messianic equation some-place. But the media, the investment houses, the suppliers, the employees, and the hopefuls all did their share to distort Cort's self-estimation.

A week after his confident statement about continuing to run the company as long as he did a good job, Cort was forced by his chiefs of staff to resign. Five of his Board members, with the support of the subsidiary presidents, told him he would have to leave the company if NSMC were to stand any chance of regaining credibility in the investment community. Their meeting was the culmination of several days of tense power manoeuvres necessary to execute the coup successfully. Next morning the New York staff was assembled in the conference room to hear Cort, trembling and voice cracking, announce his resignation.[1]

The announcement was brief, the reaction varied. Some of those present, particularly the secretaries, were taken entirely by surprise. Some may even have believed Cort's statement to *The New York Times* about resigning for personal reasons of health and much-needed relaxation. Everyone seemed to think they should carry themselves as at a funeral. In preparation for the euphemisms and false sentiment I expected to hear at this meeting, I wore my most cynical, detached frown. I heard Walther say something nice about Cort's having given so much to the company and wish him all the best; while I knew Walther must really have been thinking thoughts far less kind. Eloy and I couldn't feel sorry for Cort and his now-$15-million net worth; it seemed to me his comeuppance was deserved and overdue. Yet, of course, I did feel sorry. He *had* become used to luxuries he would likely never enjoy again, he *had* been 'an awfully nice guy' to me, he *had* been under tremendous pressure from everyone to produce, he *had* worked harder than anyone else, he *had* come to believe his own messianic creed.

Investors lost further confidence when Cort left and the stock continued its slide. Roger Walther was elected President and immediately began reducing NSMC's outrageous overhead – closing offices, firing recently wooed executives, discontinuing unprofitable programs – but trying all the while to keep up a healthy front. Having lost our original glamour, we would now bill ourselves as a terrific turn-around situation, another glamorous image of sorts to investors anxious to 'discover' winners among losers. The media that had run glowing articles in the past felt foolish and wrote extra-glaring articles now. The last subsidiaries to be acquired struggled successfully for recision of their agreements, including Cliftex and my friend Yale '68, on the grounds that they had not been informed of the material change in

---

[1] In its generally excellent article, *Fortune* said Cort was 'remarkably composed' at this meeting. I was there; he was on the verge of tears.

NSMC's condition prior to their joining up. The rest of the subs tumbled around trying to decide who should run the company, now a string of subsidiaries stripped bare of 90% of the corporate umbrella and public-relations mirage.

After two months of Walther's leadership the subsidiaries decided on Cameron Brown, head of the large Interstate Insurance subsidiary, to carry the ball. At fifty-five, Brown had the conservative image Walther, thirty-three, may have lacked. Walther had not particularly wanted the job of cleaning up Cort's mess, either. He had made his fortune selling New England Travel Company, with his two partners, to NSMC (converting much of his stock to cash); why not enjoy it? Investors saw the third Chief Executive in two months, read of S.E.C. investigations, class-action suits, and suits against the parent by NSMC's own subsidiaries! The *Wall Street Journal* even uncovered a 1964 Post Office mail-fraud investigation of a Randell enterprise. The stock eventually reached a low of $3.50 in August 1970, down almost 98% from its high less than a year earlier.

While *you* had to go pay $3.50 for a share of NSMC stock, *I* had the option to buy it for $37 a share. Actually, by the time the stock was that low I no longer had my options. I was no longer with the company and you have to be an employee for options to be valid. In March, in the midst of wild confusion, the banks withdrew their lines of credit and, of course, no one would buy the company's letter stock. Nor would healthy subsidiaries lend the parent any money, at least for a while, since they were not sure of their own legal positions. This placed NSMC on the verge of bankruptcy. I sat in Jimmy Joy's office more than once waiting to ask for money to operate our refrigerator project and heard him talk on the phone to irate creditors. They sounded remarkably like the kind of conversations we used to have freshman year in my dorm about paying the telephone bill. Only NSMC's phone bill was about 1,000 times larger and there was no one to write home to as a last resort. The strategy had to be to make payments only when the final threat of suit was made (three creditors owed $1,000 or more each, I learned, must file petitions in order for a company to be thrown into involuntary bankruptcy).

We could not meet the commitments we had made to schools to deliver refrigerators. In the case of Indiana State, I had been assured we would have the funds to deliver the 700 units that had been ordered; the campus paper announced their impending arrival. Then I was told by my boss to tell them we simply could not deliver. Then, he somehow got approval of the expenditure and told me to tell them it was on again. But I had to visit the student-government President and University Legal Counsel personally in Terre Haute to renegotiate the price of the lease now that our cost of capital had to be figured realistically. They were more than understanding and, having already collected $2 deposits from their impatient students, simply requested that we waste no time in making delivery. The refrigerators were actually loaded onto two trucks in Sydney before my boss told me that, unfortunately, we would not be able to deliver after all.

I was mortified by what we had done to the student government and the students of Indiana State. Especially when we had been billing University Products Corp. as the reliable, service-oriented company that was big enough to meet its commitments 100%. I decided to resign.

But what of the people who had invested in NSMC partly as a result of my enthusiasm? Didn't I have a responsibility to stick with the company to try to salvage something? A friend at one company that had put $10,000,000 (! !) into NSMC called me to remind me of my responsibility. I decided to stay.

One of the Directors of Harvard Student Agencies called me from Boston, told me he had heard some nasty stories about NSMC from his friends in the investment community, and told me I would be crazy, perhaps irresponsible, to stay. I decided to resign.

The concept of the company was still sound, I had a great job, in a few years my options might really be worth $400,000, things are rarely as bad as they seem, I must learn to have more patience, and so forth. I decided to stay.

I was very, very tired and so forth and so forth, and there were so many more 'so forths' on the side of resigning that resign is what I did.

I left in April 1970, just in time for my 23rd birthday.

CHAPTER TEN

Putting the Pieces Back in the Box

> Be nice to people on your way up
> because you'll meet 'em on your way
> down.
> JIMMY DURANTE

With summer 1970, approaching, I wanted to get out of unreal New York as quickly as possible and up to friendly, less frantic Cambridge. There you can walk around barefoot, feel safe, find grass, and relax a little. Enough going on to satisfy a city boy like me – but sane.

The goddamned landlord, who had earlier threatened eviction if I did not remove a peace-sticker from my door, would not let me out of the goddamned lease, which still had six months to run – even if I forfeited one or two months' rent ($365 or $730). Nor could I sublet it to the several groups who wanted to take it: only a single person or married couple without children would be acceptable. Nor would they tell me what the rent would be raised to when the lease ran out, nor give an upper limit, so I could reassure prospective sublessees. As Humphrey had by then gone off and gotten married (something about tax advantages from joint returns), mine was the only name on the lease. I finally found someone to take it for $100 a month. Some businessman I am.

I drove my things up to Cambridge in an eighteen-foot Hertz truck, which was probably sold for scrap after my battle with its transmission. I was feeling pretty cheerful, all things considered. I hadn't saved a nickel – the options had been my nest egg – but I had learned a lot. I probably couldn't have enjoyed as much responsibility anywhere else. It may be a while before I'm Vice-President of a $100-million company again, though I do try to keep my roommates off the phone as much as possible, just in case.

My only real regret was not being able to build the refrigerator company into a $100-million enterprise itself. I felt it really had that long-range (fifteen years?) potential. In the last days at NSMC I tried to work out ways to buy University Products from them; but money was tight. I went to Yale '68's banker at Bank of New York, for the fun of it, to ask for $2 million. It was an enjoyable session because we both knew at the outset there was not a chance in the world of their lending me $2 million. I did learn a little about banking, though, and he learned how to fix the old refrigerator in his basement.

Meanwhile, the new management of NSMC was trying to sort things out and assess the damage. As it turned out, the first quarter loss of $1.5 million had not cleaned the slate after all. The company decided to switch from a fiscal year to a calendar year, which enabled them to take the four-month period of September 1 through December 31 (that is, the old first quarter plus one more month) and use it as a kind of garbage can. Then the *calendar* year 1970 would have a good chance of showing profit (whereas the *fiscal* 1970 would not have). Where the Randell management had reported a $1.5 million pre-tax loss for September 1 through November 30, the Brown management showed a $4.2 million pre-tax loss for September 1 through December 31. Either things were being straightened out or December was a very bad month. If you exclude the results of the subsidiaries, then the parent NSMC showed a pre-tax loss of $5.7 million, or close to a million and a half a month.

Almost all of the original NSMC is now gone. Headquarters are no longer in Washington or New York, but in the Interstate offices in Chicago. The summer-employment guides, unprofitable media, and CompuJobs are gone. So are

139

the twenty-two account executives, the twenty-four district managers, the 700 campus reps they managed, the marketing staff, the corporate-planning staff, the corporate-marketing staff, the corporate librarian, and the public-relations staff. The freshman photo-directory and refrigerator programs are among the few core NSMC projects that were retained, and are doing quite well. Bittersweet.

At this writing, Mr $497,000, my first and third boss, is back in San Francisco, having successfully trimmed most of his assets to manageable proportions, except for the Manhattan town house, which is still on the market. My second boss, whose salary and stock option were considerably smaller than mine, is back in Toronto helping CBS diversify into new fields. My final boss, Mr On-Again-Off-Again-Refrigerator-Delivery, is running the small company he sold NSMC, and later extricated.

Maggie is flying around the world for Pan American (at least they called one of us), almost as she would have travelled had her option materialized. Because of her fluent Spanish, Pan Am loves to send her to the beaches of Puerto Rico and Spain. Her parents are now resigned not only to her hailing taxicabs, but to her sharing a midtown apartment, as well. (No Doz is still a no-no for me.)

The Canadian Personnel Manager now runs his own personnel agency in Vancouver. The Canadian head of NSMC's 700 American student reps returned to the Toronto office of Vic Chemical. The Canadian computer expert in the Washington office is computing happily in Toronto.

Roger Walther, who ran NSMC in between Cort and Cameron Brown, is back in Greenwich running his New England Travel Company, an NSMC sub. I imagine his company-furnished limousine and chauffeur are gone and that the mobile telephone has been disconnected. Disconnected also must be the mobile telephone in the identical chauffeured limousine Jimmy Joy demanded when he saw Roger's. Joy, lured from W. E. Hutton & Co. to become Senior Financial Vice-President, is back at his desk at Hutton. The opportunity for conference calls between Joy, stalled in traffic on the George Washington Bridge, Walther, racing along the Major Deegan Expressway, and Randell, 30,000 feet over Maclean, Virginia, has passed.

A sentence of before and after on each of the hundreds of people who were involved with NSMC, even if I could provide it, would turn my book into a year-book or alumni directory or something. There is certainly the feeling among many of my former colleagues and me that we were in school together. But what has happened to our Valedictorian, the Class President?

Cort, suddenly press-shy, retains over a quarter of a million shares of unregistered NSMC stock, recently quoted at $10 (unadjusted). It is anyone's guess whether he will be able to keep it – and whether he will be able to sell it. The jet is gone but high living retained, as he sets out to build Leisure Time Industries, Inc. (refrigerated trucks and music) by acquisition. He assists the Chairman of the company, based in Washington. While it is too early to tell what course Cort's career will ultimately take, it is no longer easy for me 'to imagine him the founder of a philanthropic foundation, or sponsor of medical research, or college benefactor', as *American Way* once suggested.

I haven't had any contact with Cort since he left NSMC, but I did get a call from one of his lawyers a few evenings ago as most of this book was being set in type. Mr Yoder asked me whether I remembered a letter Pontiac had sent NSMC two years ago. Why yes, I did. He wanted to know all about it – it was all a mystery to him, he said, but fascinating. I told him what I told you in Chapter 6. He wanted to know how much of that I had told the S.E.C., and I declined comment, since the S.E.C. investigation is a private one.

A few nights later Mr Yoder called back and we went through the whole thing again. What kind of typewriter was it? Where did I learn to type so fast? What time of night was it? What did Cort do with the letter? Of course, I suppose Mr Yoder knows exactly what Cort did with the letter, being Cort's lawyer, and just wants to find out whether I know what he knows.

Then Mr Yoder flew me down to Washington to discuss the Pontiac letter again, this time with two of his associates present, and I told the same story again. I drew a diagram of the office for them, identified facsimiles of The Letter that they had prepared – all the things you see on the first half hour of the Perry Mason reruns. The second half hour, the Court scene, may or may not be played. But judging from the $500 or so of legal time and expenses they have invested in talking with me, I would guess we have not heard the end of the Pontiac letter.

The recession that had begun, it seemed to me, was long overdue. Finally things were beginning to make a little more sense. The chain letters were being broken, get-rich-quick schemes were actually being labelled 'schemes', and most of the young entrepreneurs were having to adopt more reasonable timetables. Companies that had prospered by borrowing recklessly from the future found themselves up to their necks in the future. The System seemed to be correcting itself a bit. Against all the negatives of the System, one major plus seems to be its ability, sooner or later, to correct itself enough to avoid total catastrophe.

Four Seasons Nursing Homes, on which Steve Berg had bought the call, filed for bankruptcy. He should have bought a put. My Nationwide Nursing Homes, which I still can't sell, is 25c. bid, down 99%. They merged with a travel company for the obvious synergy.

The conglomerates aren't doing too much merging: 'Divesting' and 'consolidating' have come into vogue. Dolly Madison filed for bankruptcy; Jimmy Ling no longer runs Ling-Temco-Vought. With their stocks down so much, they no longer had the leverage to acquire companies at lower multiples than their own.

The franchisers have taken a beating (it's a wonder I managed to miss out on that).

Peat, Marwick, Mitchell isn't getting the best press over Penn Central, which isn't getting a very good press either. Public-relations pros are chronically unemployed as firms decide to cut costs and favour production over corporate image.

Investment bankers and lawyers who earned such fabulous finder's fees arranging acquisitions – like the man who married Resource Publications to Gulf + Western and reportedly earned $5 million in 1968 – are thinking twice about that second hydrofoil. Even graduating Harvard MBAs are having trouble getting jobs as analysts and brokers on Wall Street. No fewer that 150 brokerage houses went out of existence through liquidation and hundreds more through merger when the market turned sour.

The mutual funds are getting clobbered and my friend's flock of student salesmen has been liquidated with his company. Not to mention Bernie Cornfeld and I.O.S.

Employment agencies aren't doing awfully well, and Resource Publications is having a tough time getting people to advertise for new employees they don't need. Perhaps Dan should charge engineers $150 to publish their résumés to be sent free to big companies. Yale '68 has a business similar to Resource, with similar problems: Instead of increasing profits from $40,000 to $60,000 as projected before NSMC paid its 4,000 shares, there is a small loss this year. (When Yale '68 finally extricated his company from NSMC, he was able to keep the 4,000 shares. It may turn out to have been worth all the hassle after all, as NSMC stock begins to creep back.)

Youth Dynamics, one of NSMC's public competitors, is now quoted in the Pink Sheets at $37\frac{1}{2}$c., down from $10 when the tide was in. Class Student Services is now Class International. My hypothetical 3,000 shares of that stock are down in value from $90,000 to about $5,000.

I don't know whether my HSA friend, Max, who visited me at NSMC to tell me about a sure-fire Black Angus cattle-ranching deal, ever raised the $200 million he claimed he was after (honest!); but I did read in the *Journal* that the ranch everyone was investing in for a tax shelter went bankrupt and wound up providing a tax loss instead.

Most of the high flying technology companies crash-landed, though my only personal investment in them after Cognitronics ($60 to $4) was in a hot tip called Siltronics. By the time this one was recommended to me I had become sceptical

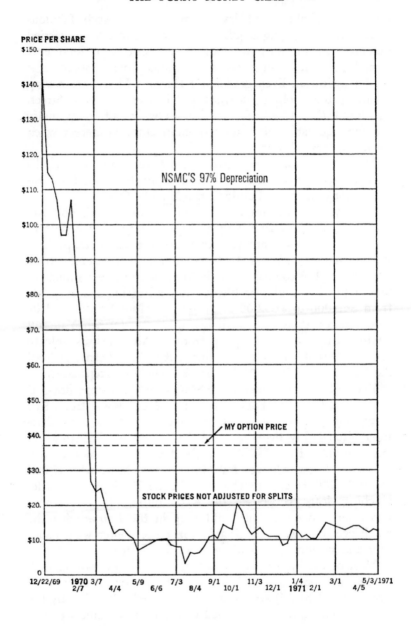

of hot tips, so I called Humphrey to buy 200 shares at $7 *only if his investigation proved positive.* He called back with more respect in his voice than usual, which isn't to say a great deal, and asked where I had heard about Siltronics. I just said I had my sources and asked what he had found out. He had found out that one of his senior people was heavily into Siltronics, and that this guy *never* bought a stock that didn't double or triple. So I bought 300 shares instead. Two weeks later, at $4.75, I asked Humphrey why Siltronics wasn't doubling or tripling. He said he would investigate, called back, and asked, 'Did you buy "Siltronics" or *"Siliconix'?"* Well, they all sound the same to me. Siltronics was last bid at about 8c. a share.

The S.E.C. and Accounting Principles Board, seeing what a mess mergers and acquisitions have made of rational economics, have finally begun to use their regulatory powers to close the loopholes. Here are four of the new rules of the game and the effect they would have had on NSMC had they been in force in 1968:

First, the S.E.C. is requiring public companies to provide more detailed sales and earnings figures *broken down by major divisions.* From the point of view of the public, it would be even better to provide the breakdown for *all* subsidiaries. regardless of size ('Will the real CompuJob please stand up.'); however, public companies argue they are already required to reveal more information than is competitively wise. In either case, analysts would have seen how much of NSMC's earnings came from insurance and clothing operations. It would have been even harder for NSMC to disguise its losing core-company operations.

Second, the earnings of companies acquired after the close of a financial period can no longer be pooled back into that period. That would have cut out $3.7 million of NSMC's $3.8 million in 1969 earnings. Instead of showing this in a footnote in the back, it would wind up in the Financial Highlights – an important change of emphasis.

Third, acquisitions cannot be accounted for as poolings of interest when the owners of the acquired company wind up with less than 10% of the stock of the parent. These would have to be accounted for as 'purchases.' Most of NSMC's poolings would have had to be purchases, with at least three deleterious results: (a) even companies acquired *before* the close of the fiscal year could not have had their full year's earnings lumped in which those of the parent – only those earnings generated after becoming a subsidiary; (b) the owners of the acquired companies would have faced tax bills they would not have with poolings, making their deals less attractive; (c) the fourth new regulation, explained below, would have applied.

Fourth, in the case of purchases, the parent can no longer just buy a company at more than its 'underlying value' without charging anything against its earnings. In other words, when NSMC purchased Colad for $2 million in cash and $1 million in stock, or when NSMC purchased Campus Pac for $6 million in cash, they did not have to show this as an operating expense. Yet when they bought a typewriter for $500 they did. Actually, the $500 typewriter might be written off $100 a year for 5 years. Similarly, Colad's and Campus Pac's assets (typewriters, machines, buildings, etc.) were written off over their useful lives. But NSMC was paying a lot more for these companies than the values of their assets ('underlying value'). The difference between what NSMC paid for a company and its underlying value was *not* written off over a period of years like a typewriter. Instead, it was shown on the balance sheets as an intangible asset called 'goodwill' – which, it was explained in a footnote, NSMC did not write off because in their opinion it lasted for ever. This was a standard practice among conglomerates and other acquisitors. For Colad $1.8 million was charged to goodwill; for Campus Pac, $5.5. million. The other $500,000 of the $6 million NSMC paid for Campus Pac represented things like typewriters that would be written off against earnings in the normal way. But the $5.5. million of goodwill would not affect NSMC's earnings.

Under the new ruling, such goodwill must be written off over a maximum of 40 years. That would have been $137,500 a year for Campus Pac, subtracted from NSMC's pre-tax earnings, which would have made the acquisition much less attractive to NSMC. The new rule makes it harder for a high-multiple stock to offer irresistible prices to prospective acquisitions. It makes it less likely that an acquisition paid for with high-multiple stock will raise the parent's earnings per share. All four of these new rules should do a lot to discourage acquisitions. The instant-earnings game may largely be over. Ideally, only those rare acquisitions that make real economic sense would be worth doing. The major loophole still will be poolings of interest allowed when the acquired company owners wind up with 10% or more of the parent stock. Originally, the Accounting Principles Board proposed a 25% cut-off, but backed down under pressure. Now even the 10% cutoff is in doubt. Reforms must be overdue to be reforms, I guess, and compromises to be accepted.

While the S.E.C. and A.P.B. were working on these problems and others (like accounting rules for franchise operations), what reforms was the Las Vegas of the East making? The only two I know of were raising brokerage commissions to small investors and increasing the special trust fund the New York Stock Exchange maintains to protect investors against brokerage-house failures. Even *Business Week* published a scathing cover article in its Halloween 1970 issue – picturing a roulette wheel superimposed on the Exchange floor. *Business Week* said:

> Bad luck is hardly explanation enough for the brokerage debacle. The current scene on Wall Street has demonstrated beyond a shadow of a doubt that many stockbrokers lack the financial stability and managerial skill they need to serve the public market. Worse, it has shown that brokers whose brochures urge investors to 'own a share of American capitalism' too often view the stock market themselves as an oversized casino. Besides doing their best to heat up their customers' speculative fever in the 1968–69 market, many brokers committed their own funds heavily in hot stocks and 'special situations', often with disastrous results. The shakeout [of brokerage firms] has raised doubts about the whole system for trad-

147

ing stocks, based on a 'self-regulating' monopoly of member brokers on the major New York Exchanges. For all the financial power of Wall Street, this monopoly is a rather precarious franchise whose continuance depends on how well it works. It does not seem to be working well at the moment, and the impression is hardly improved by recent signs of revival in the 'performance' craze [fast stock-price growth versus security and dividends; speculation versus blue chips]. 'The same stocks are making big moves,' says chairman Richard Jenrette of Donaldson, Lufkin and Jenrette, referring to the franchise stocks, computer issues, speculative oils and other go-go favourites. And Jenrette, like many other industry leaders is worried. 'It would take just one more downward lunge to create mass hatred of Wall Street,' he says.

Jenrette's company arranged a private placement of about $10 million of NSMC letter stock at $83 a share in December 1969, buying much of the stock for their own portfolio. Incidentally, you'll never guess which overly enthusiastic refrigerator renter first interested the Donaldson, Lufkin and Jenrette analyst to come and meet Mr Randell. If he keeps doing favours like that for his friends, he will shortly run out of them. As the stock was performing on down to $3.50, Jenrette's company became the first investment house in the country to go public, against the strident objections of the New York Stock Exchange. It expected to be something of a performance stock itself, originally planning to go public at a multiple in the high 20s.

I am sure there are good reasons for brokerage houses to go public, besides the personal gain to the partners. Among other reasons that are given, public money will provide these firms with the capital they need to modernize and to maintain larger margins of safety to protect their customers. Still, the idea of publicly owned brokerage houses adds just one more ripple to the fascination of Wall Street, raising it to an even higher level of abstraction.

Theoretically and hypothetically, you could be an insurance

salesman with $5,000 in the bank. The bank makes its money by investing and so phones its (publicly owned) broker to buy the stock of an insurance company. The insurance company makes its money (part of which they pay you) by investing, and happens to own shares in a mutual 'fund of funds', which only buys other mutual funds for its portfolio. One of the funds it owns has large positions in the bank, the insurance company, and the brokerage firm – which also have positions in each other. And around and around we go, without necessarily ever investing money in a nonfinancial company like a manufacturer or an airline. I'll vote for you if you'll vote for me. What if a brokerage firm recommends to its clients that they buy an insurance company whose stock is partly held by a mutual fund in which the brokerage house has an interest? The clients buy, which raises the price of the insurance company stock, which increases the value of the mutual fund, which increases the value of the broker's portfolio. We are all familiar with 'wage-price' spirals. Perhaps we will become familiar with a new kind of Wall Street spiral, also. Of course, there are two ways to spiral.

And when all brokerage houses are public, what kind of social norms will be built up between them? After all, brokers will be in the position of sending their analysts out to each other and making buy or sell recommendations about each other to their clients. If Kidder, Peabody pans Merrill, Lynch, will Merrill, Lynch still be able to provide its clients with an objective analysis of Kidder? I look forward to the day when I can call my broker and buy stock in a company that franchises other (public) companies to sell professional advice to brokerage houses with respect to which brokerage houses to buy and sell.

And when the auditors go public, and then the law firms, and the public-relations firms, and then the recently incorporated New York Stock Exchange; and then Gulf+Western buys up the stock of an auditor, which owns a public-relations firm, which owns a law firm ... I hope there will be someone left who knows how to milk a cow.

The *Business Week* article concludes:

There is no evidence that the 1960's quest for 'performance' or other speculative splurges have contributed anything more to society on balance than speculation in Las Vegas. There is ample evidence, in fact, that they can do real damage – and that brokers share the responsibility with those other Wall Street professionals du Pont's Llewellyn Young describes as '25-year-old genius fund managers with muttonchop whiskers'.

If the muttonchop brigade is indeed making a comeback, 'self-regulation' is in real danger and Wall Street's franchise, like the fast-food and nursing-home issues that fell in the bear market, is a prime short sale.

You mean my roommate went to Princeton and Harvard to become a bookie? Is his social contribution the same? His doorman would never believe it. Remember this is *Business Week* I'm quoting, not *The New Republic*. That *Business Week* has begun to talk of 'contributions to society' is an interesting sign, even if it is partly at the expense of 25-year-old geniuses with timetables to meet.

Speaking of genius fund managers, I have a question. Does one's being a genius bring him success on Wall Street – or does one's success on Wall Street make him a genius? I would say it is the latter. A book like *The Money Managers* (edited by Gilbert Kaplan and Chris Welles; New York, 1969) implies that some money managers are *really good,* and talks with great respect of the fortunes their intelligence, foresight, and coolness under pressure have produced. I have no doubt these investment-community deities *are* intelligent, farsighted, and cool under pressure. But so are Humphrey and many others who have not done as well.

Let us assume that all stocks rise or fall *at random,* and that no manner of analysis nor vision can help you decide whether they will land heads or tails. Even so, with 10,000 key money managers in New York, each with his own variation on a theory, each with his own succession of guesses – it stands to reason that a few will be *lucky* and score a long string of correct guesses. Most will bat about .500. A few will be unlucky and guess consistently wrong. The performance of money managers will conform to the same bell-shaped probability curve we learned in high school. The lucky ones will be called geniuses. And their geniusdom will be self-perpetuating, at least for a while, because people like to bet with a winner. I am sure you have noticed how little old ladies put one chip wherever the night's big winner is putting his pile. At roulette, the ball is no more likely to stop on a heavily bet number than on 00. In the market, if everyone follows the winner he will win even bigger. So it is just as important to be the first to know what a genius plans to do as it is to be the first to know what a company's earnings may be. (Chances are, the average citizen like you or me will be one of the last to get his hot tip. Unless perhaps we sign on as the genius' chauffeur. By acting on the tip we raise the stock for the genius – but who will raise it for us? Maybe if you tell all your friends . . .) Naturally, this places the genius in a pretty good seat from which to watch the horses. In order to win his favour and find out his next move, a lesser light may volunteer his hottest information on some company's earnings. Now the genius has good reason to choose a new horse.

The combination of the earnings news that leaks out later and the news that the genius is buying makes that stock a sure winner. ('What a genius that guy is to have known their earnings would go up!') After the top geniuses have bought it, some favoured clients of the New York head office are told about it, then maybe some of the branch offices and junior brokers in New York get the story, and then you and I hear about it. Who do you think is selling the stock when we rush in? The geniuses, no doubt, at a hefty profit.[1] So, if you really want to be a genius, too, short all the hot tips you get. If I had shorted instead of bought Electronics Assistance, Coburn, Cognitronics, Chrysler, Nationwide Nursing Homes, and so on – think where I'd be now!

But I have been assuming that stocks rise and fall at random.

[1] Or the insiders; in either case, I am admittedly oversimplifying.

Is that true? At least in the short run (a few months or even longer), I think it largely is. If you buy General Motors today, over the short run you are just flipping a coin. So is anyone who has no genuine inside information. Because every time GM stock is traded, the supply curve for that stock and the demand curve intersect at the price of the trade.[1] There are as many buyers as sellers. As many geniuses saying 'buy' as 'sell'. Of course not all the people buying or selling are geniuses, but most brokerage firms have constantly updated opinions about buying, holding, or selling major stocks – and these are the opinions of the geniuses. So, when you call your broker and decide with him what to do, you are following the advice of a genius. Sure, you may think there will be a strike next month – but don't you think everybody else has thought of that too? A lot of people have already sold because they guessed the strike will occur; that's why the stock is pretty low. You're guessing, like a lot of others, there won't be a strike and that it's a bargain; that's why it isn't lower than it is. If you're lucky, or if you are the chief union negotiator's daughter-in-law's bridge partner, the coin will come up heads. Or do you think you have a sixth sense, or that by watching the newsclips of the negotiators and gauging the mood of the country you *know* there will be no strike? Far be it from me to knock extrasensory perception. There are people who do seem to be able to bat consistently over .500 on the flip of a coin.

If over the long term the American economy (including GM) grows, then batting no better than .500 may still mean a nice growth in your investment – perhaps more than enough to keep up with inflation.

If I am right about the self-fulfilling power of investment geniuses, then how come they don't become increasingly venerated to the point of owning the world? Partly because competition is stiff. Other geniuses may have decided to sell what you have decided to buy, which spoils your results and

---

[1] If you think of the 'specialist,' whose duty it is to make an orderly market for shares of GM stock, as a genuine buyer or seller.

casts doubt upon your geniusdom. Alan Abelson of *Barron's* or Dan Dorfman of the *Wall Street Journal* may write an article knocking some of the issues you have made high fliers. Or perhaps this book becomes a best seller (and Haley's Comet comes three years early) and everyone begins *shorting* hot tips.

Big-money managers also have the problem of getting into and out of stocks quickly. If I call my broker to sell 100 shares of NSMC, I know he will have no trouble doing it, and at about the same price as the last trade. If a mutual-fund manager wants to sell 21,000 shares, it will take him quite a while: The faster he sells it, the lower the price he will get. What kind of bargain price would your grocer have to charge to get you to buy 50 times your normal supply of eggs? What's more, he may have bought letter stock at a discount – and the 'letter' requires him to keep this stock for a period of years as an investment. The genius must have a good idea of the *long-run* prospects for a company and for the economy – and these are not greatly affected by the news that he has bought the stock. He starts guessing too.

So they don't own the world, but they own what you might think is an unfair chunk of it.

My point is not that Wall Street and public ownership should be abolished. Though I wouldn't rule it out, I don't even begin to know enough economics to start theoretically tampering with the country's financial structure. But I do dare to suggest that the system strongly favours the insider, the financial club, try as the S.E.C. may to protect us. And that we are foolish to invest in speculative issues expecting not to lose our money. (You can tell how speculative a bet you are placing partly by the multiple of earnings you pay.)

Instead, we should picture the market as a special roulette table – the same 36 numbers, red and black, but instead of a 00 where everyone loses and the casino makes its 3%, there is a + + where everyone wins, and the economy has grown by 3%. If you invest in a hot tip, you are putting your money on No. twenty-four and would seem to have only two chances in thirty-seven of winning – No. twenty-four or + +. But the chances aren't even that good, because analogous to the casino's magnetized ball is the market's favouring of those close to the top and the annoying tendency of bubbles that inflate to 20 times their original size in a year's time to burst or be suspended from trading. Only with a truly remarkable discovery – a tremendous oil field, the telephone, the laser – does it make economic sense for people to make a fortune overnight. Buying a string of youth-oriented companies just doesn't cut it. How often will you be one of the first in on such a discovery?

If instead of putting all your money on one of thirty-six numbers, you keep betting black (i.e., blue chips), you are likely to come out a little ahead in the long run, but you won't make your fortune in three to five years.

I have nothing against gambling by those who can afford to do it; and I recognize the economic importance of speculators in the market. But I'm not sure the get-rich-quick kids, myself included, had a full understanding of just how much gambling they were doing or how the odds were stacked. By coming to expect less we may get more.

CHAPTER ELEVEN

Prospectus Perspective

> The love of wealth is therefore to be
> traced, as either a principal or
> accessory motive, at the bottom of all
> that the Americans do; this gives
> to all their passions a sort of
> family likeness. . . .
> *Democracy in America*
> ALEXIS DE TOCQUEVILLE

It was beautiful to be back in Cambridge, though it had changed a lot in the six years since freshman-orientation week. As freshmen we had been required to wear ties and jackets to meals; we were forbidden to entertain guests in our rooms after seven in the evening. As a freshman I had literally never heard of marijuana or mescaline. SDS was just beginning and looked as though it would be another super-boring political group, working for seconds on dessert and maybe pass/fail courses. Well, you know what I found when I returned to Cambridge this year.

I was admitted to the Harvard Business School again, but still wasn't sure I should go. Every Harvard MBA I spoke to advised me unequivocally that I *must* go, would be out of my mind not to. Every non-Harvard-MBA told me I should save the money and time, that I could learn just as much in two more years on the outside. Is there some magic to the Business School one can only appreciate by experiencing it? Or is it simply natural for those who have invested so much time

and money in the MBA, and who want it to carry the most possible weight, to describe it as 'indispensable to any sort of success in business'? After all, if they can convince us of that, they
will have eliminated all the non-MBAs from the competition
for success, and have that much better chance themselves.
Just as naturally, the non-MBAs must defend their shot at the
top spot. How much of the Harvard MBA thing is a mutual-
admiration society, an exclusive social club, backed by first-class
public relations?

While I was trying to figure out whether to go back to
school, I needed a job to support the electric bill for all my
gadgets. Yet another young entrepreneur from Harvard
Student Agencies had started a glamorous technology firm he
invited me to join, with a $20,000 salary (which goes far in
Cambridge) and, needless to say, a stock option. The company
was planning to go public shortly, etc., etc . . .

I was suspicious because the prime-mover of this company
was a big guy who spoke very quietly, but in very dreamy
terms. He spoke of things as virtually completed facts when
they were only possibilities. He was surrounding himself with
expensive overhead that had just graduated in the top 5%
of the Harvard Business School class, ready to cash in. He
named his company National Information Services when it
had sales of less than $1 million, all in the Boston area. A
lot of those national sales came from a near-bankrupt, anti-
quated printing company he had acquired for stock. And so on,
and so on.

This time I was a little smarter than usual. I accepted the
job but did not cancel my place at the Business School. I
figured if the company were all I had been told, it would make
sense to pass up Business School again and join those who say
it really isn't worth the time and money. But if things were
as empty as they seemed, this would be an ideal summer income before joining the ranks of those who attest to the indis-
pensability of the Harvard MBA.

I told him that he couldn't afford to hire me, that I knew
nothing about information services, and that it all sounded very
much like another NSMC—but that if he really wanted to,

and would guarantee my salary in writing, I would be glad to come. As it turned out, without the written guarantee I would have had to settle for about 50c. on the dollar. Tight money and failing investor confidence in the summer of 1970 brought this company back down to earth, too.

Scratch one more young mogul.

Business School, I have had the couple years practical experience in the real world you recommended, even if it was not quite what you had in mind. Thanks for saving my place. 'Frankly, I think a Harvard MBA is indispensable to any sort of success in business. . . .'

After all this frantic experiencing of the real world close up, I had several weeks to climb out of my 3-piece suit and step back a little. What had been NSMC's place in the world? What was really going on?

In the midst of a crisis-ridden world, whose salvaging probably requires the utmost in human talent, energy, patience, and self-sacrifice, a small group of talented, energetic, young men – already tremendously privileged – gathered for the purpose of extending their privilege even further. As healthy, well-educated, upper-middle-class Americans (and Canadians) these men, including yours truly, already lived more comfortably than 99.9% of the rest of the world's inhabitants. But to talent and energy they added impatience and self-aggrandizement in order to live more extravagantly than 99.9% of their fellow Americans, which is to say more extravagantly than 99.999% of the rest of the world. They did so out of no perverse or evil inclinations. Rather, their culture pointed the way. The way is up, and up is more, and more is good. The American economy will grow for ever, with minor setbacks, and that is good.

Specifically, these young men spent their talent and energy buying companies that filled various functions in the economy. Rearranging the ownership of these productive units and putting them together under one corporate structure cost a great deal in energy and expertise, but produced nothing. They worked hard to shuffle the deck, they reapportioned wealth from others to themselves, but they did not produce anything, and there were still only fifty-two cards in the deck.

Besides buying other companies they cut down forests and made the trees into paper and used a great deal of labour and expertise to print offers for such things as useless summer-employment guides on the paper and scatter the paper as unwanted litter all over the country. About half a billion separate pieces that had to be picked up, brought to collection centres, and burned, putting unhealthy gases into the air. Some of the papers were in fact effective as a means of communication between producers and consumers, and served a purpose; but the same results could have been achieved far more efficiently, cutting down fewer trees, ladening fewer postal couriers and student representatives, creating less litter, polluting less air. The statistical proof of this was the unprofitability of the effort. Yet the inefficiency and unprofitability of their activities did not cause them personal discomfort; they were able to convince people they should be rewarded. The inefficiency and unprofitability of their activities were instead shared by human society as a whole: Human and natural resources wasted that could have been put to good use, a finite livable environment cluttered and polluted that could have been left just a little more livable.

These privileged young men flew around in a private plane whose construction and operation required staggering natural and human resources, resources that wound up contributing nothing to society but air pollution and air traffic, while planes of almost equal convenience flew just as fast to the same cities with half their seats empty.

The great wealth they accumulated seemingly came from other fabulously wealthy people (by world standards); in fact this was not altogether the case. For one thing, investors like the General Mills Pension Fund and the Harvard Endowment Fund represented the interests of less wealthy working people and of higher education, respectively. For another, the millions of dollars spent nonproductively on rent and furnishings and travel and communications and administrative, legal, accounting, and public-relations talent – all this came out of the public pocket. The less efficient the economy, the less you get for your dollar, the less you get for the work you do. This is not just America's waste and America's loss; it is the world's.

How could the nonproductive NSMC resources have been better allocated? The office space and furnishings could have been used by the Foster Parents Plan to expand their operation. The forests could have been left standing to preserve the environment, or the trees could have been used for free textbooks or birth-control leaflets for underdeveloped areas of the world. The lawyers could have been working to improve the ponderous legal system that favours the rich, or could have been defending the poor. The administrators and accountants could have been managing the welfare system with less waste. The public-relations and sales types could have been out selling everyone on a better world. The student reps could have been assisting public-school teachers or playing volleyball with prison inmates. Where would all the money have come from to pay for the rent, the trees, and the salaries? Society was already paying this money, though it did not appear specifically on a Congressional appropriation bill. The resources are still there for society to use.

I wonder whether NSMC was an isolated case of misallocated human and natural resources, or whether virtually all conglomerates are wastefully constructed and held together by unnecessary top layers of business bureaucracy. It might be argued that no misallocation would have occurred if NSMC had played by the rules. While it is important for the S.E.C. to decide whether the public was defrauded, it is also important to consider that it all *could* have happened without breaking rules. Wall Street fads and funny money acquisitions are both legal and commonplace.

Such were my thoughts when I looked to see what the NSMC bash had contributed to society. When I read *The Environmental Handbook* – edited by Garrett De Bell (New York, 1970) – I became even more distressed. First it points out that while we were trying to figure ways to triple NSMC's earnings for ever, there was another exponential growth problem perhaps more pressing. If the population of the earth continues to grow at the present rate, in 900 years there will be one square foot of surface for every 100 people, including oceans and ice caps.

Either the death rate must increase – war, famine, plague, mass suicide, suffocation; or the birth rate must decrease – when the world becomes so miserable that no one would want to bring a child into it. In my freshman economics class we laughed at Malthus, who had said population will always grow as fast as the food supply allows, keeping man for ever at the bare subsistence level. Infinite natural resources had proved him wrong. But now they say our resources (space, air, water, fuel), though very great, are not infinite. What will prove Malthus wrong this time?

Let us make the optimistic assumption that we lick the population problem short of war or plague or famine. The environmentalists still aren't satisfied. We are at the point, they say, give or take a few years, where the incremental advantage of another dollar of gross national product is outweighed by the corresponding incremental disadvantages of resource depletion and waste disposal. Especially if that incremental dollar represents another unit of horsepower in some young entrepreneur's GTO. According to these scientists, we are borrowing from the future just as recklessly as Cort did. We are looking for infinite growth on a finite planet – impossible as a successful chain letter, but enticing if you are among the first to sign up.

(Are we beginning to feel the pinch? Buying power per capita has actually *decreased* over the last couple of years. According to that same economics course, when demand (population) increases and supply (resources) decreases, prices go up and less is consumed.)

'Standard of living,' I read in *The Environmental Handbook*, is competing with 'quality of life'. The *Wall Street Journal*, they hope, will someday say, 'The GNP took a turn for the better this month as it resumed its descent, interrupted last month by what appears to have been a statistical aberration. The White House issued a statement taking credit for this encouraging development.'

Do they mean we should actually produce and consume

less to live better? If not less, differently. Tractors instead of tanks, $100 billion in needed products and services for neighbouring countries instead of $100 billion to maintain and expand our arsenal, schools instead of the SST, recreation areas instead of oil-depletion allowances, systems that entail more labour and less waste (like returnable bottles).

Maybe the American economy won't grow for ever and it's time to short the blue chips?

Thanks to *The Environmental Handbook*, I'm living much more simply now – or is it thanks to my recently acquired poverty? Not only does this seem to be a requirement of improving the environment – it saves money. It is thus an easy philosophy to adopt.

I'm not going to any extremes. I am never hungry, never cold or wet, never dirty, never lacking good medical attention, never denied stimulating entertainment. I still live better than most Americans and much better than almost everyone else. I am no less happy.

Did I sell my tapedeck because I am 'poor' now or because I've changed? Is my generation renouncing super-consumerism? Which way do we want the growth curves to curve? Is this why my friends and I are having trouble deciding which way is up and what to work for?

Are the scientists right? If they are, will America believe them? If so, will American business be able to cope with such new values and ground rules? How? What of the tenet that a business can only be healthy when it is growing? These were among the questions I had in mind as I entered Harvard Business School.

CHAPTER TWELVE

Next Time I'll Divide
Myself Into a Million Shares

Round like a circle in a spiral,
Like a wheel within a wheel;
Never ending or beginning,
On an ever spinning reel . . .
From the lyrics of *Windmills of Your*
Mind
MARILYN AND ALAN BERGMAN

I thought the rooms at Harvard College were nice. Most were
suites of large rooms, many with fireplaces, one bedroom per
student if you had any luck at all, and a john for the suite.
Very comfortable. I expected Business School rooms to be
even better. I had heard about the daily maid service and
assumed the rooms were built with executive aspirations in
mind. Perhaps a sophisticated dictating system built into the
wiring; surely an executive refrigerator bar, one or two large
rooms per student, private bath, sauna, air conditioning, panel-
led-wall-to-panelled-wall carpeting; perhaps our names cut into
those little Formica nameplates you see in most offices. I wasn't
sure whether Morris Hall would have a doorman, and whether
the elevator would be attended or self-service – I figured I had
better check things like this before moving in.

I got an advance look at the typical double room (there
are a few singles, but they are hard to get): A shared bedroom with the two beds running parallel and two feet apart,

closet space for two sports jackets or one overcoat each, and one University-supplied chest of drawers each, an ample eighteen inches wide. The other room is the study/living room, just large enough for two desks, two chairs, a radiator (no room for that in the bedroom, bring blankets), and a shelf just the right size for the text materials you will buy. Telephones are allowed, but only with short cords. Long cords are a hazard (tripping over them, hanging yourself with them). The University rulebook explains that trunks are not allowed above the first floor, but trunk rooms are provided and are open occasionally. Presumably you bring your trunk to the first floor landing and unpack on the stairs.

The prevalent assumption is that these double rooms were built as singles – they would make good singles – but as enrolment grew they became doubles. I decided to try to get a single.

The lady in charge of room assignments suggested I look at the singles before I apply for one. That same day, as the last item on the news, they showed a full-grown man whose hobby was contorting his body to fit inside a small aquarium. No one else could do it, not even his children. That man would be comfortable in one of the single rooms at the Business School.

The doubles and singles come in different colours. Some are institutional green, some institutional grey. There are wall-to-wall linoleum and pipes running around the ceiling. And there really is maid service.

Through a great stroke of luck I heard of a *double* room that was vacant (it was above the furnace room or something; the noise drove out the former occupants). I asked the rooming lady if I could have it all to myself. She suggested I go near it before signing up. While I was walking over there, I realize now, she must have called Buildings and Grounds and instructed them to run the furnace in low gear for a few minutes. When I got to the room, I could hear it – like the soothing hum of an air conditioner. Sign here.

As I write this, Boston is experiencing a cold spell. The furnace is running around the clock at full tilt. My earphones

163

are not equal to the task. I have to sit with my ear to the telephone to hear it ring, which means at my desk, since I couldn't get a long cord. Silver lining: The furnace drowns out the noise of my compact refrigerator.

I heard about this great room from L. E. Simmons, my former refrigerator salesman, who is now one semester (and several thousand dollars) ahead of me at the Business School. Part of all that money he made goes to his Harvard tuition; part goes to eight-year-old Adalberto Valdez, whom he adopted through the Foster Parents Plan; and part I am gradually winning from him at Foosball, which is my sole means of support at this time.

I have long since spent the money I earned writing an article for *New York* magazine about my fling in New York. The one that pictured me on the cover inside a bubble about to burst. The day the magazine came out, NSMC stock dropped 30%, which is to say two points. That was just as 1970 was drawing to a close.

The annual report for calendar 1970 was a simple black-and-white affair, sober in tone. The reduction in corporate staff from 160 to fewer than ten people was noted. 'NSMC, the parent company, is a holding company. Previous activities of the parent are conducted through subsidiaries.' Subsidiary profits for 1970 were enough to absorb the losses the parent incurred while it was being pruned and such 'extraordinary charges' as a million-dollar loss incurred in subletting unneeded office space and disposing of plush furnishings. There was even $382,593 left over as net earnings for the year, or 12c. per (unadjusted) share.

We might assume that 1971 will not be burdened with parent company losses and extraordinary charges, and that earnings will be substantially higher. This must be what Wall Street assumes as the stock trades around $10 to $12 a share, or about 100 times 1970 earnings. Yet at least two major problem areas remain to be resolved.

First, there are some legal problems. There are class action suits and breach of contract suits noted in the annual report. It is also noted that the former owners of NSMC's Houston ring manufacturer are suing to get their company back. It accounted for $339,552 of NSMC's $382,593 net 1970 earnings. And it is further noted that if the S.E.C. finds NSMC violated the Securities Act of 1933 or the Securities Exchanges Act of 1934, 'it may have both civil and criminal liability'.

Second, there is a problem with goodwill. About $10 million in goodwill remains on the balance sheet, and the new management has decided to write it off over 30 years – even faster than the new accounting rules require. Yet that may not be fast enough for the $5.2 million portion attributable to Guest Pac (whose major activity is Campus Pac). In the years before 1970 Guest Pac had shown fat profits. Hence the fat price NSMC was willing to pay to acquire it, hence the fat goodwill on NSMC's balance sheet. In 1970 the Guest Pac management were replaced, including the President of Campus Pac.

He has set up 'Campus Kit' and claims to have signed exclusive contracts with hundreds of the college stores that used to handle Campus Pac. Anyway, in 1970 Guest Pac lost $453,787. Peat, Marwick refer specifically to this problem in their opinion letter, noting that 'management is of the opinion that no reduction of this amount [the $5.2 million of goodwill] is necessary at this time'. And, after all, in America everyone is entitled to his opinion. Should management be forced to write this amount off all at once instead of over thirty years, there would be an extraordinary charge against earnings of $5.2 million, or about $1.60 a share (unadjusted).

Although morale could be better, the worst seems to be over. There is evidently enough cash in the till to pay Cameron Brown, the Chief Executive Officer, his $175,000 salary. And to pay John Davies, 30-year-old Secretary and General Counsel and about the only important holdover from the Randell management, his $60,000 salary. *Fortune* reports that NSMC is the 846th largest industrial corporation in the U.S.

All things considered, it is reasonable to expect NSMC's string of nineteen subsidiaries, which by and large were profitable before being acquired, to keep NSMC in the black, on the theory now finding favour that $1+1+1+1=4$. If I were a Wall Street analyst, I think I would value the earnings I expected NSMC to show in the coming year (exclusive of extraordinary items) at fifteen to twenty-five times, bearing no grudge. It seems like that kind of wallet.

The market in general has been doing well, as the Dow Jones climbed back from 630 to the 900s again. Does that mean the Dow Jones 30 industrial companies are producing 50% more than they were nine months ago in the summer of 1970? Or that moving into Laos has the opposite effect of moving into Cambodia? Or does it simply mean that Wall Street has convinced itself of what it wants to believe?

New issues are coming out again. Among them, 'Insurance brokers [as distinct from insurance companies], once mostly private partnerships, have been going public at almost a frenetic pace, and have been using their shares to grow by acquiring smaller brokerage firms.'[1] Surely *this* fad won't be like all the others.

One big market for insurance brokers lately has been the liability insurance for which corporate officers, directors, and auditors have been clamouring. The public should feel secure in the knowledge that these responsible men are insured against irresponsibility. We should not mind the fact that we are the ones paying their insurance premiums (the auditors pass on their increased insurance costs to their clients, who pass on their increased auditing costs to their customers – you and me.)

A former NSMC colleague visited me at the Business School as I was drafting this chapter and told me his own insurance-company anecdote. He recalled how he had been flying in the Lear Jet with Cort and Jim Joy, the Financial V.-P., from a meeting with a prospective acquisition (a chain of movie theatres that derived most of its profits from a handful of theatres that charged $5 per showing and required viewers to be at least twenty-one years of age). Cort and Jim were discussing the impending Interstate merger and Jim pointed out how beautifully unfathomable were the financial statements

---

[1] *Business Week*, March 13, 1971.

of an insurance company. 'We'll be able to do all *kinds* of things!' or words to that effect. If this kind of thinking rubs you the wrong way, please consider two things. First, of course, all of us make statements and think thoughts that are not intended for publication. Second, and more important, *this is the way the system works.* Insurance-company financial statements *are* unfathomable and there are some perfectly legal ways to take advantage of that fact. A Financial Vice-President would have to be dull or altruistic not to consider such things – and he is surely not being paid to be dull or altruistic. Any good Financial Vice-President would have thought the same thought.

The same kind of argument, I think, can be made in 'defence' of anyone I seem to be 'attacking'. Including me, including Cort, including the p.r. writers, the accountants, the directors, the investment analysts. In general, I think the individuals involved played the game within the rules as they saw the rules. In general, I think the rules they knowingly broke were the kind they felt 'everyone' breaks, like kids smoking marijuana. It may in fact be that more serious laws or regulations were clearly and intentionally violated; I don't know. The important thing, though, is that it all *could* have been built *without* breaking any laws; by stretching, but not exceeding, the limits of acceptability of the system. In my opinion, these limits are not drawn tightly or clearly or forcefully enough.

An individual business in a competitive environment can't be expected to be self-regulating. It would be unfairly penalized for its good intentions. However, if all businesses are regulated equally, by their trade association or an arm of the government, then the competitive balance is maintained and the public interest is served. Only when the rules of the game are truly shaped in conformance with the public interest will the social responsibility of business, as economist Milton Friedman says, be profits.

I apologize for getting theoretical. It is because I am now back in the ivory tower trying to figure things out.

Classes here at the Business School are more fun than my

college classes were. Perhaps it is because I am interested in the subject matter. I tend to think, though, there are other reasons. The outstanding faculty teach with more energy and humour than their counterparts across the river. The courses are all taught by the 'case method', which means class discussions of real business situations rather than theoretical lectures. And, mainly, the classroom chairs swivel around and rock back and forth. No doubt you have noticed how much easier it is to wait for an ice-cream soda on a spin-around fountain stool than in a stationary chair. Well, ends of classes have always seemed to me like ice-cream sodas.

Our finance class is taught by a man who was appointed a Director of the Pennsylvania Company by the Bankruptcy Court. One of the readings he assigned was an article called 'The Earnings Per Share Trap,' by Marvin M. May, published in the *Financial Analysts Journal* during NSMC's first month as a public company:

> Sometime during each generation the magic of the chain letter is rediscovered. The phenomenon has reappeared this time in a very unusual and unlikely locale and form; it has seduced the investment community. While it is generally agreed that chain letters cannot create wealth, it is well recognized that they are a very effective means of transferring and redistributing wealth. . . .

When I first read through the article I assumed it had been plagiarized from my Chapter 5. Then, remembering that it had been written three years before Chapter 5, I could only wonder why the financial community had paid no attention to it.

In another class we had a case on corporate jets, noting their inefficiency, and a case to decide whether or not TWA should add crêpes suzette to their menu to steal some market share from American. Most of us decided to decrease the number of competing airlines instead. We are a less conservative class than, say, the class of 1968.

In a class designed to show the value of planning by the

critical-path method, we discussed the case of a Florida home builder with about $2 million in sales. We didn't know which one it was; generally all the case names are disguised. At the end of the class we were asked whether we thought this company, despite its dreadful planning and control, would attempt to expand – yes, most of us did – and if so, whether we thought it would fall flat on its face – yes, most of us did. 'Okay, Barry,' continued the professor, 'do you want to take the last five minutes to tell us how your family's business has done since the case was written?' So *that's* why Barry is always talking about the construction industry! (The company had grown to $80 million of profitable sales.)

For our Administrative Behaviour course we were asked to 'go out into the field' – that is across the river to Harvard Square – to observe some human behaviour. Pierre and I were told to observe the human behaviour at Design Research, a four-storey see-through department store on Brattle Street specializing in expensive furniture, fabrics, and frivolities.

Pierre had just arrived from Brussels and was not used to everything American. (About a fourth of the class comes from outside the U.S.) He asked me countless questions and I, who have an answer for everything, cheerfully filled him in.

I spotted an electric pencil sharpener on the counter – a really neat-looking one cased in a transparent cylinder so you could see what was going on inside – the motor and stuff. Very handsomely designed, with a small hole on the top, off to the left of centre, into which you insert the pencil, I explained to Pierre, who had never seen an electric pencil sharpener before.

He was fascinated as I went on to explain how a light probably flashed on to tell you when the pencil point was just right. He took it from me, commented on the $30 price tag, and pressed one of the panels on the side. Flame emerged from the hole you put the pencil in and I caught a faint odour of lighter fluid.

Pierre took this opportunity to light his pipe, and having, I suppose, asked just about every question he could think of, asked me no more the rest of the day.

We have a course called Environmental Change and Business Decisions, taught by George Lodge, who ran against Teddy Kennedy for the Senate in 1962. When we were discussing urban transit, he explained, 'I've asked my brother Henry to sit in today. He heads the Massachusetts Bay Transportation Authority.'

Lodge seems to feel that we can no longer trust the old notion that the whole will take care of itself while all the parts fight like crazy for their own interests. He thinks that more planning, co-ordination and regulation are needed if that whole is to be a success; that the revolving doors might jam if everyone thinks only of himself in rushing to get out of a burning building. Most of the class appears to buy much of this social awareness, although one classmate keeps proposing the Survival of the Fittest as the ideal form of social organization. Of course, it's what we do when we get out that counts, not what we say in class.

Through all of the classes and cases and conversations I try to figure out what to do when I graduate. I really enjoy business and reject the idea that socially concerned people should avoid the Establishment. That will only perpetuate the status quo. If we tell businessmen to act in a socially responsible way and tell people who act in a socially responsible way to do something more 'useful' than business, we will lose socially responsible businessmen as fast as we can convert them. Although standard of living is threatening quality of life, American business has, for all its imperfections, certainly provided us more of both than any other large group of people has ever enjoyed.

On the other hand, there are many nonbusiness activities that are awfully appealing, as well.

The problem is not as simple as Establishment or anti-Establishment, technopalace or commune. It is steering some kind of satisfying middle course.

So far I have come up with two attractive possibilities, though the first is not awfully practical:

I have thought of turning professional, travelling around the world giving lessons, playing in tournaments, and making

TV commercials. However, I fear the formation of a full-fledged Foosball fraternity is a far-fetched futuristic foos-fantasy. In a more realistic vein, I have considered incorporating myself and going public. Why should I work for the next thirty years to earn a small amount each year when I could go public now at thirty times earnings and get it all 'up front'? It is common knowledge among the Harvard MBAs on Wall Street that a Harvard MBA will earn a lot of money in his lifetime. Therefore, if I went public on the projection that I would earn $5,000 a year after expenses, with the possibility of earnings growth over time, I imagine Wall Street would buy my stock. That would give me $150,000 to work with. I would use $5,000 of this to pay the first annual premium on a $150,000 officer's liability insurance policy. Then I would issue myself a $145,000 bonus and go off to the beach somewhere. Wall Street would sue for their investment, charging gross mismanagement, and would win. Luckily, I would be insured. Having issued myself a bonus equal to my total working capital, my corporation would quickly go bankrupt. However, I could repeat the process every two years under a different corporate name, because Wall Street forgets.

POSTSCRIPT – APRIL, 1972

For the year ended December 31, 1971, NSMC reported sales of $73.3 million and an operating profit of $1.9 million, or 15c. a share. Of course, that doesn't include a special charge of $12.3 million for the write-off of goodwill and other assets. Remember Campus Pac?

On February 3, 1972 the Securities and Exchange Commission broke the silence of its two-year private investigation with a 46-page complaint against, among others: NSMC, Randell, John Davies (the corporate counsel), James Joy and Bernard Kurek (the former financial V.P.s), Cameron Brown (then NSMC President, now replaced), Peat, Marwick,

Mitchell & Co., and White & Case. The naming of a law firm in an S.E.C. complaint was unprecedented.

The S.E.C. alleges that the NSMC affair was a 'fraudulent scheme'. The complaint cites unbilled receivables that were never to be billed or received, including 'a purported sale made to Pontiac . . . for approximately $800,000'. The complaint cites 'materially false and misleading' press releases, speeches, reports, proxy statements, and financial statements.

As for why anyone would purchase a loser like CompuJob at a profit to NSMC, the S.E.C. alleges: (a) the transaction was included in 1969 statements even though negotiations did not commence until 1970; (b) the purchasers were not personally liable on the $225,000 note they gave NSMC, which was secured by 4,500 shares of NSMC stock; (c) the purchasers got those 4,500 shares from Randell in exchange for some stock in a firm the purchasers set up, called Strider Oceanic Corp.; (d) NSMC agreed to continue to run CompuJob for another year and would absorb any losses incurred; (e) NSMC would hold the purchasers harmless against any losses, expenses, or damages connected either with the purchase of CompuJob or the sale to Randell of Strider Oceanics stock; and (f) none of these rather elaborate arrangements was disclosed in NSMC's financial statements.

For the transgressions the S.E.C. alleges, they ask the court to enjoin the defendants from doing this kind of thing again. And they would like NSMC to restate its 1968, 1969 and 1970 financial statements. Harsh treatment? A deterrent to others considering a financial fling at the expense of the public?

On April 23, 1972 NSMC stock was $1.12 bid, or, unadjusted for the two splits, $4.50 – just a shade beneath the issue price of $6 a share exactly four years earlier.

National Student Marketing Corp., now headquartered in Chicago, is a shadow of its former self but seemingly out of the legal thicket at last—it is largely a schoolbus-and-insurance company. Its stock, still traded over the counter, has recovered from its low of around 25 cents to nearly $2 a share.

Cortes Randell served eight months of an eighteen-month federal-prison term. He is now back in McLean, Virginia, in the same house on the Potomac, where he is vice-president of a barter organization called The Washington Trade Exchange. He has found Christ and appeared on at least one religious TV broadcast.

In late November, the SEC charged Randell with looting more than $300,000 from a Virginia-based finance company he controlled, as well as violating the law in connection with the sale of securities in that company.

Randell denied the charges.

He was convicted on five counts of mail fraud and seven counts of securities fraud, four counts of interstate transportation of funds obtained by fraud, and one count of making a false statement to the Veterans Administration. "Being an entrepreneur is dangerous," he told the *Washington Post* in 1987, three years after he had returned from serving four years of a seven-year prison term. (His first term was in minimum-security Allenwood Federal Prison Camp. His second, in medium-security Petersburg Federal Correction Institution.)

In 1984, shortly after his release, he signed on as the sales and marketing guy for what would become Federal News Service, a Washington-area transcription service. His partner, Richard Boyd, had recently been convicted on charges of overbilling the Reagan administration for transcribing presidential news conferences, among other things. Not a multi-million-dollar defense contractor type of overbilling—those guys almost never go to jail—just $13,000. But overbilling is overbilling, and when Boyd eventually got to spend a few months in Allenwood himself, he charges, Cort pretty much made off with the transcription business.

Nonsense, Randell told the *Post*; Boyd would get his share, even though Randell deserved all the credit for building their Federal News Service. (It's a service on which reporters, lobbyists and others rely for almost instant transcripts of government briefings, hearings and speeches.) Boyd sued Randell and Randell's wife. Randell and Boyd's ex-wife sued Boyd—it gets messy. But by 1990 the *Washington Post* was referring to Randell as the founder of Federal News Service, which was thriving, with no mention of Boyd. As of 1993, the litigation continues. No trial date has been set. If it weren't for the litigation, any number of potential suitors might be interested in acquiring it. There's even been some talk that—hold onto your hats—it might go public. The castle on the Potomac is gone, though Cort and Joan are reported to be living very nicely. Maybe one of these days they'll be able to buy it back.

In his 1987 interview with the Washington Post, Randell reflected on his past. "The Lord has let me be successful in business," he said. "I have gotten some bad advice and probably made some bad choices in terms of people, but I've been more careful this time." One wonders what bad advice or bad people advised him to change Pontiac's "we are not planning" letter to "we are now planning"—could this have been a bad choice he made all by himself?—but he seemed to feel he had done nothing wrong.

"We built a big, strong company," Randell told the Post, saying that lots of companies were selling for high multiples of earnings in those days, but that only his was singled out for prosecution.

NSMC never did go broke. Someone who had bought NSMC stock for 3/8 of a dollar ($1.50 in pre-split terms), its lowest asking price at the bototm in late 1970, would have realized about $7 when the last pieces were sold off (mostly on the sale of the insurance subsidiary to American Express). Which just goes to show Cort bought a few pretty hardy companies—and that you can make as much on the rebound, scavenging for something no one wants, at 3/8 of a buck, as you can when the music is sweet and everybody wants in. Riding a stock from 3/8 to 7 is to realize an 18-fold gain. That's even better than you would have done buying the stock at 14, when NSMC first opened for trading in April 1968, and selling it at that top, at 144. Of course, it would have taken longer and been less fun. Investing is never as exciting as speculation.

So here we are in the fall of 1993, with the Dow Jones Industrial Average at an all-time high, and stocks like Snapple valued at $3 billion and 100 times last year's earnings, but growing fast. Snapple, is doubtless the next Coke, and cheap at $3 billion. But out there somewhere, I'm convinced is the next National Student Marketing Corp. Dozens of them, in fact. And always will be.